TOMORROW'S MARKETS
Global Trends and Their Implications for Business

D1709658

World Resources Institute

United Nations
Environment Programme

World Business Council for
Sustainable Development

2002

ORDERING PUBLICATIONS

WRI

Hopkins Fulfillment Service
PO Box 50370
Baltimore, Md 21211-4370
Tel: (1 410) 516 6959
Fax: (1 410) 516 6998
E-mail: hes.custserv@mail.press.jhu.edu

Publications may be ordered from WRI's
secure online store: **www.wristore.com**

WBCSD

WBCSD, c/o The Sales House
Tel: (44 1423) 357 904
Fax: (44 1423) 357 900
E-mail: wbcsd@thesaleshouse.com

Publications are available on WBCSD's
website: **www.wbcsd.org**

UNEP

SMI (Distribution Services) Limited
Unit L, Gunnelswood Park
Gunnelswood Road
Stevenage SG1 2BH
Hertfordshire England
United Kingdom
Tel: (44 1438) 748111
Fax: (44 1438) 748844
E-mail: enquire@smibooks.com

Publications may be ordered from UNEP's
online bookshop: **www.earthprint.com**

DISCLAIMER

Publications Director: Hyacinth Billings, WRI
Design: Alston Neal, Barbieri & Green, Washington, DC
Printer: CifiLaboureur Imprimeur, Paris, France

Photo Credits: Don Doering (pages 3, 33, 36), Molly Hewes (page 60), Andrew Katona (pages 48, 50, 51), Alston Neal (page 42)

ISBN Number 1-56973-497-6
Library of Congress Control Number 2002101675.

Partners' Foreword

onathan Lash
RESIDENT
orld Resources Institute

Our three organizations join with this publication to communicate the trends that are shaping the global business environment. The future's successful companies will be led by people with the vision to combine the case for sustainable growth with personal and social values to create a powerful business case for change and innovation. *Tomorrow's Markets* shows that future growth will be in the competitive space in which winners are those that create value without environmental costs.

The shadows of environmental degradation, poverty, and lack of economic opportunity lie across the regions of the world that are fertile ground for ethnic conflicts, hatred, and violence. The private sector has a more important role than ever before to develop products and practices and to support policies that protect and restore the environment, that eradicate poverty, and that create a fair and transparent society. The challenge of the future is to choose a course that satisfies the market requirements for growth, maintains the natural balance that sustains our economies, and meets the needs and rights of global communities awakening to new dreams of health, prosperity, and peace. *Tomorrow's Markets* is a call for action and a sign of opportunity for the tremendous creative and innovative capacity of the business community.

jörn Stigson
RESIDENT
orld Business Council
r Sustainable Development

Many cases can be made for sustainable development; yet, being a business council, we have worked to define the business case for sustainable development. The business case is an entrepreneurial position. It looks at how business can be more competitive by being more sustainability-driven. It covers themes such as eco-efficiency, the role of global and capital markets, corporate social responsibility, transparency, innovation and technology, sound environmental management, and new partnerships, to name a few.

We live in a world of rapid change and our future is uncertain. Business leaders need to identify the fundamental signals that influence their future success and drive their innovation.

The WRI report, produced in partnership with UNEP, looks beyond daily preoccupations and identifies key trends that shape the business agenda. It does this in a concise and lively format.

As encapsulated in its title, we hope the facts and trends presented in this report will help to shape the markets of the future by providing companies with intelligent information to devise better corporate strategies and identify new business opportunities.

laus Töpfer
ECUTIVE DIRECTOR
hited Nations
nvironment Programme

Access to reliable and timely information is increasingly important in our globalised world. For policy-makers and business leaders alike, recognising the trends that shape the marketplace and understanding the reasons behind them are more important than ever.

This is why UNEP is pleased to join forces with the WBCSD and WRI in producing this new publication, which builds on UNEP's Third Global Environment Outlook report to be launched later this year. We have concentrated on making the links between environmental, economic and social trends.

The World Summit on Sustainable Development is fast approaching, and 2002 promises to be a landmark year for environmental protection and poverty alleviation. With increasing interest in new public-private partnerships, the Summit in Johannesburg is expected to address the relationship between industry and the environment, and innovative ways of dealing with complex socio-economic issues.

Sustainable development also makes good business sense. The facts and trends presented in this new publication make it clear that we cannot go on as we have thus far. I hope they will also help business leaders to better understand the inter-relationships between environment and development issues, and therefore respond more effectively to the enormous challenges before us.

Preface by Michael Porter HARVARD BUSINESS SCHOOL

What is the relationship between corporate strategy and societal issues such as the environment, poverty, health, population, and international development? Business leaders have a tendency to see "social" concerns as having little relevance to competing. Instead, these fall under the headings of corporate citizenship or corporate philanthropy, or are left to managers to address as matters of individual conscience.

It is becoming more and more apparent, however, that treating broader social issues and corporate strategy as separate and distinct has long been unwise, never more so than today. Seeing strategy narrowly leads to missed opportunities and bad competitive choices. It can also cause managers to overlook potential competitive advantages.

The same disconnect between social and corporate is also common among leaders in the social sector. There is a tendency to view firms as adversaries — not as allies in advancing social causes. Yet we are learning that the most effective way to address many of the world's most pressing problems is to mobilize the corporate sector in a context of rules, incentives, and partnerships where both companies and society can benefit.

In modern competition, economic and social policy can and must be integrated. Consider some examples. Controlling pollution and the emission of greenhouse gases is often viewed by firms as a social issue, and resisted as driving up the cost of doing business. Environmentalists, who often believe companies seek to profit from polluting, see their role as advocating regulations to compel companies to install available abatement technology whatever the cost.

> We are learning that the most effective way to address many of the world's most pressing problems is to mobilize the corporate sector where both companies and society can benefit.

Yet virtually all corporate pollution is a sign of economic waste and the unproductive use of resources, and can be addressed with better technology or improved methods. Forcing companies to install abatement technologies is usually the wrong approach; the better approach is product or process innovation. The same is true with the use of energy, the cause of most greenhouse gas emissions.

Innovative corporate practices in the area of the environment, then, will often enhance internal competitiveness. Products that address environmental scarcities will also have enormous market potential. This means that companies should see environmental protection as an opportunity, while environmentalists need to recognize that progress on environmental improvement will be most rapid if they work cooperatively with companies. Governments in developing countries must understand that strategies of environmental degradation lead to continued poverty, not successful economic development.

Similar conclusions apply to other social concerns areas such as racial and ethnic discrimination, worker health and safety, and training. For example, looming labor shortages in advanced nations give companies strong incentives to hire and train minorities, as long as social advocates do not create unnecessary legal and regulatory risks of employing such individuals.

Not only can corporate and social needs be integrated, but the success of the developing world in improving prosperity is of fundamental strategic importance to almost every company. The world economy is not a zero sum game in which one country's success comes at the expense of others. There is enormous potential for growth if many countries can improve in productivity and trade with one another. There are huge unsatisfied human needs to be met in the world, and demand will only increase as more nations become more prosperous.

Social and corporate also come together in the controversial areas of globalization. Social activists, not just companies, have a major stake in the openness and fairness of the international trading system. The evidence is compelling. Compared to local companies in developing countries, foreign companies bring higher environmental standards, pay and treat their workers better, and employ safer workplace practices. If social activists have improving these conditions as their true objectives, they will work with international companies rather than oppose them

> Not only can corporate and social needs be integrated, but the success of the developing world in improving prosperity is of fundamental strategic importance to almost every company.

The volume provides a fascinating and important foundation of data that will help to highlight and help leaders capitalize on these opportunities. It catalogs the market opportunity in addressing social needs, and the payoff to successful international development. It reveals the competitive advantages and economic benefits of innovations to improve environmental performance and better utilize scarce resources. It highlights the importance of democracy and the role of transparency to achieve such win-win progress.

Both the corporate and the social sectors will need to adopt new mindsets. This book provides an invaluable tool for doing so.

Michael E. Porter is the Bishop William Lawrence University Professor, based at Harvard Business School. A University professorship is the highest professional recognition that can be given to a Harvard faculty member. Professor Porter is a leading authority on competitive strategy and international competitiveness and is the author of 16 books and over 75 articles.

Contents

Connections

Roles and Responsibilities

People and Tomorrow's Markets

☐ **Population**

◼ **Wealth**

☐ **Nutrition**

◻ **Health**

◼ **Education**

SERVING SOCIETY

Future consumer markets and labor will be
concentrated in the fast-growing, emerging
markets where small and large enterprises
will find profitable opportunities to help meet
health, education, and nutrition needs. These
markets will favor businesses that partner
with government and civil society to serve
basic needs, enhance human skills, increase
economic capacity, help remedy inequities,
and conserve the environment.

We live in a world of continued population growth, even as fertility rates decline worldwide. In 25 years the population is estimated to reach about 8 billion — a third larger than today.[1] Population dynamics are at the root of almost every world trend shaping tomorrow's markets; population growth affects the environment and the health, nutrition, education, and wealth of the world's citizens. In the next 20 years, populations will shrink or barely grow in the high-income countries (Gross National Income (GNI) per capita ≥ US$9,266) and most of the world's citizens will be born in low- (GNI per capita ≤ US$755) and medium-income economies (GNI per capita US$756-9,265).[2] To maximize the potential of low- and medium-income labor and consumer markets will require the development of a skilled work force and products and services tailored to people's basic needs and to the needs of an expanding middle class (see **Wealth**). Developing countries will need to nurture their domestic industries to serve their own population and today's multinational companies will need to develop appropriate strategic, technical, operational, and marketing competencies to operate in these new markets.

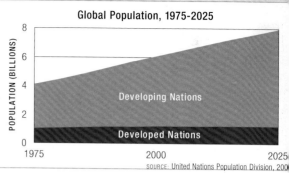

The World's Population Is Growing

Global Population, 1975-2025

SOURCE: United Nations Population Division, 200

Earth's population reached 6 billion in 2000 and is projected according to the United Nations' medium variant projection, to reach approximately 7.9 billion by 2025 and to be near stable at around 9.3 billion in 2050.[3] Declining fertility rates have significantly reduced annual population growth rates, which peaked at 2.04% in 1965–70 and declined to 1.35% between 1995 and 2000. In the next 20 years, 98% of the projected population growth will be in developing countries.[4]

Expanding population in developing regions will create large markets dominated by the young.

Facts

- More than 80% of the world's people currently live in developing countries and 85% will live in developing countries by 2025.[5]

- 2.4 billion of today's total population of 6.2 billion people are children and teenagers.[6]

- Two out of five people in the world live in either China or India.[7]

- World fertility rates have declined from about 4 children per woman in 1975 to less than 3 children per woman in 2000.[8]

- Between 1990–1995, 40% of population growth in high-income countries was due to migration, while in low-income countries, migration reduced population growth by about 3%.[9]

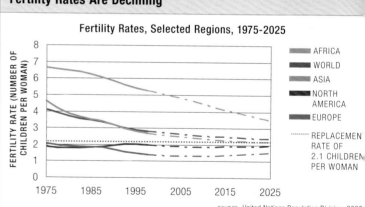

Fertility Rates Are Declining

Fertility Rates, Selected Regions, 1975-2025

AFRICA
WORLD
ASIA
NORTH AMERICA
EUROPE

REPLACEMENT RATE OF 2.1 CHILDREN PER WOMAN

SOURCE: United Nations Population Division, 2000

Fertility rates are low in the developed countries and falling rapidly in most developing regions. Nonetheless, demographic momentum — today's large generation of children reaching their reproductive years — means that world population will keep growing for several more decades before world fertility rates reach the steady state replacement rate of 2.1 children per woman. Fertility is below replacement levels in Europe and North America. In most developing regions, fertility rates are still above replacement, though falling fast, thanks in part to family planning and education (see **Education**). Africa is the only region of the world in which fertility rates are not expected to fall to replacement level by 2025.[10] In many African countries, fertility rates currently range from five to seven — although deaths from HIV/AIDS will offset some of the resulting population growth.[11]

Population Growth Creates New Markets

World Population by Income Group, 1970-1999

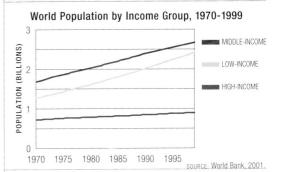

SOURCE: World Bank, 2001.

Rapid population expansion in low-income and medium-income countries is contributing large numbers of potential workers and consumers to the world's economy. The steady population in high-income countries means that few additional workers and consumers are being added in these countries.[12]

2.4 billion of today's total population of 6.2 billion people are children and teenagers.

Changing Age Structures Will Bring Social And Economic Shifts

Population Distribution by Age, 2000 and Projections to 2020 (in grey)

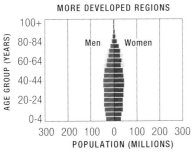

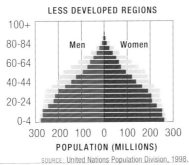

SOURCE: United Nations Population Division, 1998.

Young people predominate in the current and projected age structure of the developing world. The working age population in developing countries is projected to rise to 70% by 2020 — an increase that could help fuel developing country economies, but also drive emigration or result in high unemployment (see **Labor**). In contrast, the low birth rates and high longevity in industrialized countries will lead to a bulge of people aged 50-90 in 2020.[13] These large elderly populations will place demands on national systems of pensions, healthcare, and personal services that will be supported by the productivity of smaller populations of younger people.

Implications for Business

Population dynamics are both a major force shaping the terrain of international markets and are at the root of society's greatest economic and social challenges. The growing population of young people in developing countries represents major new labor and consumer markets for business, particularly as traditional developed country markets shrink with declining populations and become characterized by an increasing proportion of the elderly. To build developing country markets, large and small national and international enterprises must support stable employment and supply people with products and services that meet basic needs, are affordable, accessible, and are culturally appealing.

The world is getting wealthier and the economies of poor countries are developing, yet within regions and within countries, income disparity is often great and the absolute number of people living in poverty is very high. Low- and middle-income countries often lack the resources to eliminate problems such as rapid population growth, inadequate education, high incidence of malnutrition and poor health, corruption and political instability, and destruction of natural resources. High levels of income inequality limit the poverty-reducing effects of growth and it has been estimated that high inequality countries will need to grow twice as fast as low inequality ones to halve poverty by 2015.[1] To make stability and prosperity a global reality will require protecting the resource base and ensuring that people in low-income countries have the opportunities and the freedoms (see **Democracy**) to raise their living standards and to fully participate in the international community and global marketplace.

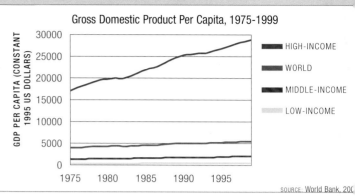

The World Is Wealthier...

Gross Domestic Product Per Capita, 1975-1999

- HIGH-INCOME
- WORLD
- MIDDLE-INCOME
- LOW-INCOME

SOURCE: World Bank, 200

World economic output has averaged 2.9% annual growth since 1975. Citizens in th high-income countries saw their incomes grow on average much more rapidly tha those in middle- or low- income countries, leading to an even larger worldwide incom disparity today than there was in 1975 (see **Consumption**). Since 1975, per capit gross domestic product (GDP) has increased by about 280% in East Asia and th Pacific, 66% in North America, and 23% in Latin America and the Caribbean, whi GDP per capita has decreased by 17% in Sub-Saharan Africa (see **Democracy**).[2]

Global wealth is rising
but the income gap grows wider.

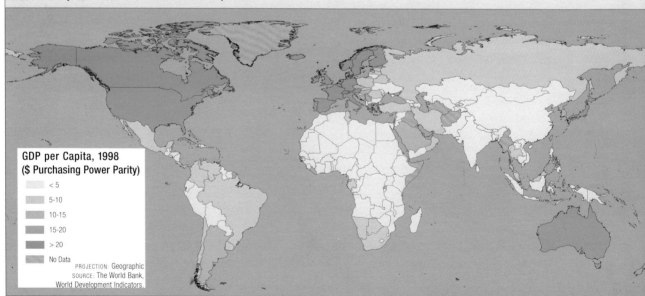

World Map of Gross Domestic Product, 1998

GDP per Capita, 1998 ($ Purchasing Power Parity)

- < 5
- 5-10
- 10-15
- 15-20
- > 20
- No Data

PROJECTION: Geographic
SOURCE: The World Bank,
World Development Indicators.

The map above shows gross domestic product in five GDP categories for the world's countries in 1998. A comparison of this map with the map of projected water scarcity in 2025 (see **Water**, page 37) and the map of projected urban growth in 2015 (see **Urbanization**, page 41) hints at the convergence and connection of social, economic, an environmental challenges faced by many countries in Asia, the Middl East, Africa, and South America.

Facts

World economic output more than doubled in the past 25 years, to about US$33 trillion by 1999.[3]

In the 1990s, household consumption (the market value of all goods and services purchased by households) grew annually at 3.7% in low-income countries, 4.1% in middle-income countries and 2.3% in high-income countries.[4]

The world is 78% poor (average purchasing power parity income less than US$3,470 annually), 11% middle income, and 11% rich (average purchasing power parity income more than US$8,000 annually).[5]

The richest 1% of the population receive as much income as the entire bottom 57%; i.e., less than 50 million richest people receive as much income as 2,700 million poor.[6]

Poverty Remains A Major Problem

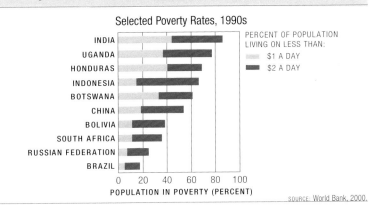

Selected Poverty Rates, 1990s

PERCENT OF POPULATION LIVING ON LESS THAN:
$1 A DAY
$2 A DAY

SOURCE: World Bank, 2000.

Although the number of people living on less than the purchasing power equivalent of $1 per day in developing and transition economies fell from 28% to 24% of the population between 1987 and 1998, the absolute numbers of people in poverty hardly changed.[7] The situation is even worse in countries such as India where over 80% of the population lives on less than $2 per day and over 40% on only $1 per day. Data in the above graph are from the most recent year available and are converted to international dollars to equalize the purchasing power of different currencies.

The world is 78% poor, 11% middle income, and 11% rich.

RELATED TRENDS

Consumption	22
Democracy	50
Urbanization	40

Inequality Within Countries Also Persists

Distribution of Income by Quintile of Population, Selected Countries

HUNGARY, 1998

INDIA, 1997

UNITED STATES, 1997

BRAZIL, 1996

SOURCE: World Bank, 2001.

In addition to the unequal distribution of income among countries, distribution within countries is also unequal. For example, the poorest fifth of Brazilians receive only 3% of the income while the richest fifth have access to more than 60%. The poorest fifth of the United States receive 5% of the national income while the richest 20% receive about 46% of national income.[8]

Implications for Business

Long-term business growth and fair access to opportunity requires bringing millions of people into the global economy and narrowing the income gap between citizens in high- and low-income countries. The expanding middle- and lower-income consumers represent potential markets, and developing affordable goods and services for those markets can drive innovation, new business models, and business growth. Examples include emerging markets for photo-voltaic generators and renewable energy for small scale applications, fuel efficient stoves, water sanitation and personal hygiene products, mobile communications, and Internet access in low-income country markets. However, the conditions for free markets may be threatened by widening income inequalities and economic failures that foster violent conflict and erode democracies and the rule of law. Enduring worldwide progress — economic as well as social — depends on alleviating poverty.

Although world food supplies have grown faster than population, millions of people who might be engaged in learning, commerce, and building a stronger society are malnourished and spend their lives on basic survival. The most widely recognized cause of malnutrition is poverty — lack of the means, land ownership, and knowledge to produce or obtain food. Yet there are other environmental and social factors at work, too, including land scarcity and degradation, water scarcity, drought, and war. Political factors strongly influence the distribution of food and subsidies and trade protection may also hinder the development of resource-efficient agriculture and food distribution. Meeting food needs in poor countries will require new and creative investments in agriculture and food production and distribution. The international business community has and will be called upon to play both a commercial and a humanitarian role in solving the problems of malnourishment.

Progress In The Fight Against Hunger

Undernourishment in Developing Countries, 1979-98 and Projections to 2015

UNDERNOURISHED POPULATION, ANNUAL AVERAGE (MILLIONS)

Legend:
- LATIN AMERICA & CARIBBEAN
- MIDDLE EAST & NORTH AFRICA
- SUB-SAHARAN AFRICA
- ASIA & PACIFIC

SOURCE: FAO, 20█

Improved technology, higher incomes, and better policies have helped enhance nutritic for many who could not meet their daily nutrition needs (undernourished) and th decline in the number of undernourished is projected to continue in the comir decades. However, where incomes have been stagnant and population growth rapid, a in Sub-Saharan Africa, the actual number of malnourished people has grown. Countri with improved nutritional status also had larger increases in secondary school enro ment of women.[1] Under-nutrition and food insecurity is also persistent in the Centr Asian states of the former Soviet Union due to economic crises.[2] The disparity in supplie of protein-rich meat and milk products is particularly acute between rich and poor.[3]

Millions are malnourished amidst an abundance of food.

Facts

- Although individual consumption levels vary enormously, the world produces enough protein to supply everyone with about 75 grams per day.[4]

- In 1998, 791 million of the 826 million undernourished people lived in the developing world.[5]

- Worldwide, about 160 million children under the age of five were malnourished in 1995, a total that is expected to decline only about 15 percent to 135 million by 2020.[6]

- Iron deficiencies in children and adults result in economic losses equal to 1% of GDP in Pakistan, and 2% of GDP in Bangladesh.[7]

Childhood Nutrition Varies By Region

Number and Percentage of Children Under Five that are Underweight, 1995-2000

UNDERWEIGHT CHILDREN (MILLIONS), ANNUAL AVERAGE AND PERCENT OF TOTAL

- Sub-Saharan Africa 31%
- Middle East & North Africa 17%
- South Asia 49%
- East Asia & Pacific 19%
- Latin America & Caribbean 9%
- World 28%

SOURCE: UNICEF, 200

Twenty-eight percent or about 170 million of the world's children under five years ol are severely or moderately undernourished.[8] Malnourished children are more vulner able to many childhood diseases, including diarrhea and measles.[9] Research ha found that improved food availability and women's education is the best approac to reducing child malnutrition (see **Education**).[10] Childhood undernourishment an its link to impeded development and a lifetime of health problems has long-terr negative effects on the productivity of families and economies (see **Health**).

In 1998, 791 million of the 826 million undernourished people lived in the developing world.

Is The 30-Year Increase In Grain And Cereal Yields Ending?

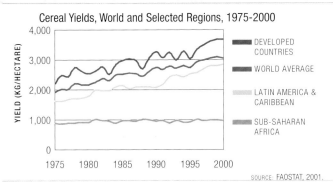

Cereal Yields, World and Selected Regions, 1975-2000

SOURCE: FAOSTAT, 2001.

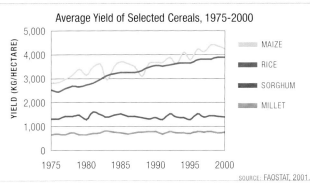

Average Yield of Selected Cereals, 1975-2000

SOURCE: FAOSTAT, 2001.

Between 1961 and 1990, global cereals production increased 120%. The average yield per hectare rose 90% in developed countries and 120% in developing countries, though yields in developing countries remain about one third lower than in developed regions. However, to meet nutritional needs, production increases are shared by a growing population and yields per capita grew about 60% in developed countries and only about 10% in developing countries from 1961-1990. In Sub-Saharan Africa, per capita cereal production for food, feed, and seed has actually fallen 11% since 1975. African farmers often cannot afford inputs like fertilizers, and many traditional African crops, such as millet and sorghum, have not been the focus of public and private research as have maize and rice (see **Agriculture**). Since about 1995, cereal production and yields have been relatively stable worldwide, raising concerns that the modern agricultural inputs of fertilizers, irrigation, mechanization, selective breeding, and pesticides have reached their limits to increase production.[11]

RELATED TRENDS

Agriculture	34
Ecosystems	32
Health	16

Feeding The Family Strains Some Budgets

Food Expenditures as a Percentage of Per Capita Income, Selected Countries

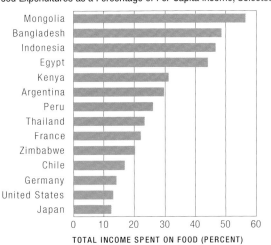

TOTAL INCOME SPENT ON FOOD (PERCENT)

SOURCE: World Bank, 2001.

In many developing countries, food purchases account for a huge proportion of family income, often 40-70% in the poorest countries.[12] While there are no standards by which to measure welfare based on expenditure, it is likely that when food exceeds one third of family income, health, education, leisure, transport, and housing suffer (see **Wealth**). The poor are also extremely vulnerable to food price shocks that can occur when crops or markets fail or when governments become unstable. Better nutrition, in turn, can mean greater income at the household and the national levels.

Implications for Business

Economies and individuals cannot achieve their potential unless adequate nutrition is met. Food production, transport, and distribution is one of the largest business activities in the global economy but the food system is neither environmentally sustainable nor yet meeting all people's needs. Eliminating hunger will require major policy changes by national governments and the international community, and private sector investments in the food system. General private sector investment in economic development creates jobs and higher incomes to allow people to purchase food. For the broad array of industries involved directly in the food supply chain, supporting the development of markets in countries with high malnourishment is a critical contribution to worldwide economic growth and opportunity.

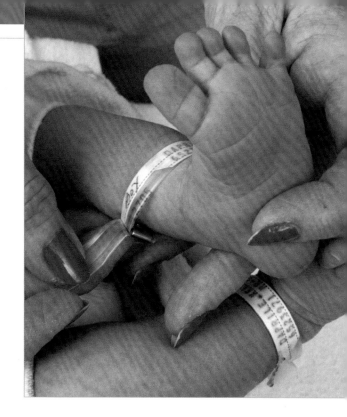

Despite a century of rapid progress in improving human health, many people do not have access to basic healthcare and basic hygiene to protect them from infectious agents in the environment. Infectious diseases conquered long ago in the industrialized world continue to kill millions in poor countries and to thwart the growth of fledgling economies. Many infectious diseases are exacerbated by environmental degradation ranging from urban air pollution and flooding, to contaminated water sources (see **Water**). The newest preventable worldwide killer is Acquired Immune Deficiency Syndrome (HIV/AIDS). In the 20 years since it was identified, HIV/AIDS has killed more than 21 million people and devastated the social fabric of some of the world's poorest nations.[1] HIV/AIDS is a grim reminder of the cost of disease: AIDS undermines economies by decreasing life expectancy, killing productive adults, raising costs for training and healthcare services, and reducing labor productivity due to absences for illness, caring for family members, and funerals.

Life expectancy rises,
yet preventable disease continues to limit development.

Facts

- World life expectancy rose from 47 years in 1950 to an estimated 66 years in 2000.[2]

- Cholera, almost eliminated by water treatment in the industrialized countries, is on the rise in poor countries. About 371,000 cases per year were reported in the mid-1990s, up from 100,000 per year in the 1980s.[3]

- Over 8 million new tuberculosis cases occurred in 2000 causing an estimated 2 million deaths, most aged 15 to 45; 99% of deaths occurred in the developing world.[4]

- More than 40 million people worldwide are living with the human immunodeficiency virus (HIV).[5] About one third are aged 15 to 24, on the brink of their most productive years as workers and citizens.[6]

- Tobacco is responsible for one in 10 adult deaths today. The figure is expected to be one in six in 2030 — more than any other cause of death. Seven of ten of these preventable deaths will be in low- and middle-income countries.[7]

World Life Expectancy Is Rising

Life Expectancy by Region, 1995-2000

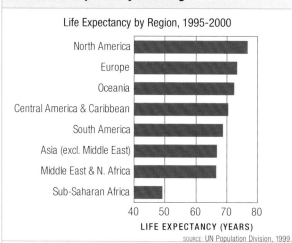

LIFE EXPECTANCY (YEARS)

SOURCE: UN Population Division, 1999.

The regional variation in how long children can expect to live is still very large as are differences within regions. Children born today in Eastern Africa can expect to live less than 50 years, compared to more than 75 years for their North American counterparts.[8]

On Average, We're Living Longer

Life Expectancy, World and Selected Countries, 1970-2010

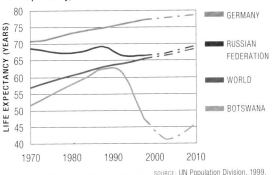

SOURCE: UN Population Division, 1999.

Average life expectancy has increased continuously since the 1950s, rising by about nine years since 1970. However, economic hardship and infectious disease can quickly halt or reverse progress. Life expectancy in Botswana was rising until HIV/AIDS took hold; declines in the Russian Federation are due to the impacts of economic downturns on healthcare, standard of living, and social institutions.

Disease Takes A Heavy Toll In Developing Countries

Cause of Death in Selected Regions, 1999

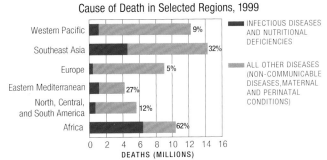

NOTE: The number to the right of each bar indicates the percent of all deaths from infectious diseases and nutritional deficiencies.
SOURCE: WHO, 2000.

Improved nutrition, sanitation, water treatment, and insect control have virtually eliminated many previously deadly infectious diseases in wealthier countries, and education, medicines, condom use, and clean needles control the spread of HIV/AIDS. In many developing countries, where disease vectors are more prevalent and where governments cannot afford investments in public health and education, infectious diseases remain major causes of death (see **Water**).

World life expectancy rose from 47 years in 1950 to an estimated 66 years in 2000.

RELATED TRENDS

Emissions	26
Water	36
Mobility	42

HIV/AIDS: A Deadly Trend

Leading Infectious Killers Worldwide, 1998

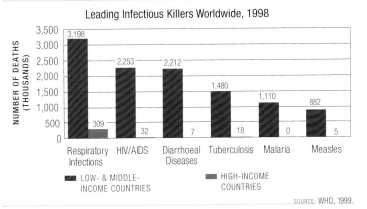

SOURCE: WHO, 1999.

HIV/AIDS has joined the list of the top causes of death worldwide such as diarrhea, tuberculosis, and measles which together claim almost 6 million lives annually.[9] The human and economic toll of HIV/AIDS in the most affected regions is staggering. Of the 36.1 million people infected with HIV worldwide in 2000, 25.3 million live in Sub-Saharan Africa and 5.8 million in South and Southeast Asia. The devastation caused by AIDS has been especially severe in Sub-Saharan Africa where nearly 70% of adults and 80% of children with HIV/AIDS live. The southern cone of the African continent has adult prevalence rates of at least 20%.[10] Good data is still scarce from most Asian countries, but AIDS deaths are rising rapidly in India, China, and elsewhere; deaths from AIDS among 15-49 year olds in Asia are projected to grow 57% from 2000 to 2005.[11]

Implications for Business

The health of employees, customers, shareholders, and other stakeholders is a central concern for corporations because health directly affects productivity. The expansion of travel and trade provides new routes for the spread and re-emergence of infectious diseases and can turn seemingly national or regional health crises into global ones. HIV/AIDS has exposed the critical linkage between health and labor productivity and how disease deprives struggling societies of desperately needed know-how and labor in business, government, and education.[12] Improving health in the developing world means improving access to healthcare, improving health education and family planning services, providing widespread immunizations and clean water, and creating economic incentives for preventive medicine and sanitation. This is a strategic opportunity for the private corporations in sectors such as pharmaceuticals, health services, water infrastructure, and water sanitation who hold the technical solutions to major public health problems. However, business failure to act on an issue of public health that is within its means can itself become a damaging political and public issue.

Education helps ensure that people have the skills to be productive workers, informed consumers, responsible citizens, and stakeholders in government and business. An educated population produces and earns more, has lower fertility rates, is more effective in maintaining family health, and has greater choice in life decisions. While primary education is widespread, many children in emerging economies do not have opportunities for advanced learning, and in some regions girls have far less access to secondary education than boys. Within regions and countries with high levels of average school enrollment, there are often significantly under-served populations. The more advanced skills and learning afforded by secondary and tertiary schooling are ever more important as the world economy becomes more knowledge- and service-intensive.

Literacy Rates Are Rising

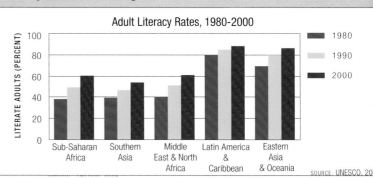

Adult Literacy Rates, 1980-2000

SOURCE: UNESCO, 200

World literacy rates have been rising for two decades, reflecting the increasing access primary education. Literacy rates in Europe and North America are virtually 100% (not shov in figure). Almost 90% of adults can read in Eastern Asia and Oceania, Latin America, and t Caribbean. Literacy rates in much of the rest of the world lag behind; Southern Asian literac rates are only slightly above 50%. The worldwide gender gap in primary education shrinking — by 1997, more than 95% of girls attended primary schools, compared to 88 in 1980. But still nearly two thirds of the world's 880 million illiterate adults are women.[1] Litera is also a proxy for the level of education of a country's potential labor force (see **Labor**).[2]

Primary education is widespread, but opportunities for learning elude many.

Facts

- 113 million children are out of school, 97% of them in less developed regions and 60% of them girls.[3]

- One of every five adults — a total of 880 million adults — is functionally illiterate. This is a dramatic improvement over 1970, when one of three was illiterate.[4]

- Enrollment rates for 6-14 year-olds is 52% lower for the poorest households, than for the richest households in Senegal, 36% lower in Zambia, 49% lower in Pakistan, and 63% lower in Morocco.[5]

- Much of the economic success of the "Asian tigers" may be due to their governments' commitment to public funding of primary education as the foundation of development.[6]

- The few developing countries that participated in the Third International Mathematics and Science Study had the lowest scores at Grade 7 in the study; quality of education is as important as enrollment itself.[7]

Many Are Denied The Chance For Advanced Learning

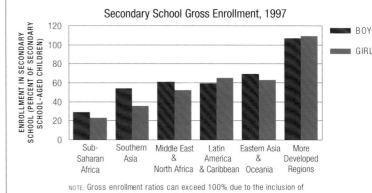

Secondary School Gross Enrollment, 1997

NOTE: Gross enrollment ratios can exceed 100% due to the inclusion of over-aged and under-aged students.

SOURCE: UNESCO, 1!

In many developing countries and marginalized areas in the developed world, there ar still major disparities in academic achievement that result from factors including inade quate teacher training and under-funding of schools and that prevent students fror obtaining the knowledge and skills needed to function as productive citizens and workers While essentially all children receive secondary schooling in more developed regions, on about 60% of young people in Eastern Asia, Oceania, Latin America, and the Caribbea receive secondary schooling; Southern Asia and Sub-Saharan Africa enrollment rates ar just 45% and 25%, respectively. The gender gap in secondary school enrollment is rela tively small in East Asia, but significant disparities in access to education remain in Sout Asia, the Middle East and North Africa, and Sub-Saharan Africa.[9]

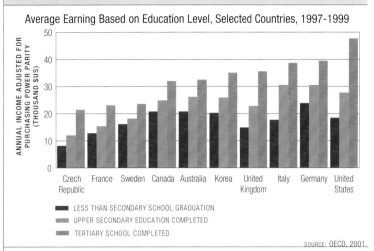

Educational Disparities Create An Income Gap In All Countries

Average Earning Based on Education Level, Selected Countries, 1997-1999

ANNUAL INCOME ADJUSTED FOR PURCHASING POWER PARITY (THOUSAND $US)

Czech Republic, France, Sweden, Canada, Australia, Korea, United Kingdom, Italy, Germany, United States

■ LESS THAN SECONDARY SCHOOL GRADUATION
■ UPPER SECONDARY EDUCATION COMPLETED
■ TERTIARY SCHOOL COMPLETED

SOURCE: OECD, 2001.

Education provides people with opportunity to excel and opens the doors for economic advancement. While many social and economic factors influence this relationship, the relationship between advanced education and income is very strong (see **Wealth**).[10]

One of every five adults — a total of 880 million adults — is functionally illiterate. This is a dramatic improvement over 1970, when one of three was illiterate.

RELATED TRENDS

Labor	46
Communications	44
Accountability	52

Female Education Helps Catalyze Economic Development

Fertility Rates vs. Percent of Girls Enrolled in Primary School, 1990s

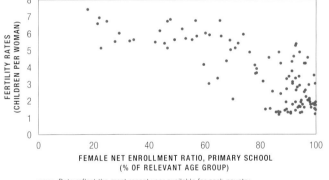

FERTILITY RATES (CHILDREN PER WOMAN)

FEMALE NET ENROLLMENT RATIO, PRIMARY SCHOOL (% OF RELEVANT AGE GROUP)

NOTE: Data reflect the most recent year available for each country.

SOURCE: World Bank, 2001.

Girls who receive primary education tend to have lower maternal mortality, fewer children, and healthier families later in life.[11] In Asia, Africa, and Latin America, women with seven or more years of schooling have two to three fewer children than women with three or less years of schooling.[12] Smaller families lessen the economic burden upon women and release time and resources for parents to provide greater investment into the rearing and education of each child and more opportunities for women to enter the labor force (see **Labor**).

Implications for Business

Education enables people to get jobs, maintain family health, increase personal income, reduce unwanted pregnancies, protect their rights and civil liberties, and have greater choice in decisions that affect their lives. Countries in which the work force lacks basic skills are at a competitive disadvantage in the global marketplace, particularly as markets change from a production and manufacturing base to a knowledge and service base. Businesses have a direct stake in the educational systems in the communities in which they operate. Additional investment and resources are required to ensure that those entering the labor force will have the relevant skills to be productive workers in modern businesses. In order to marshal these investments and resources, new partnerships are needed between public and private sector organizations to ensure that people are educated for relevant and marketable skills.

Innovation

☐ **Consumption**

☐ **Energy**

☐ **Emissions**

☐ **Efficiency**

MORE VALUE WITH LESS IMPACT

The rise in world affluence holds promise
for better lives and also comes with
significant risks to ecosystems if prevailing
patterns of consumption, energy production,
and waste persist. The need to reduce
consumption and waste creates new
opportunities for business to grow while
at the same time helping people,
economies, and ecosystems through the
innovation of less wasteful processes,
and life-enhancing goods and services.

Consumption

Growing income has allowed people to expand their consumption of everything from meat and dairy products, computers, energy and paper to refrigerators, televisions, and automobiles. The greater consumption of food, housing, clean water, and transportation is essential to relieving poverty in many nations. However, the high consumption of the world's affluent consumers can have a negative impact on ecosystems disproportionate to their numbers. Today's model of intensive use of raw materials and resources undermines ecosystem function and runs the risk of overwhelming the planet's capacity to absorb wastes (see **Emissions**). Meeting the needs and desires of all people while preserving resources requires innovation of new technology and business models. Business can lower the resource intensity of the production of consumer goods, while improving their top and bottom lines and meeting consumer demand with sustainable products and services. Consumers themselves can drive change by favoring companies that produce goods and services that protect, conserve, and renew the environment (see **Ecosystems**).

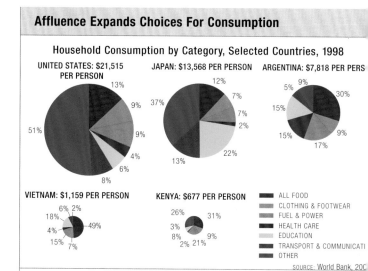

Affluence Expands Choices For Consumption

Household Consumption by Category, Selected Countries, 1998

SOURCE: World Bank, 200

People in high-income countries spend a much smaller percentage of their resources on the basic necessities of life, enabling them to purchase life-enhancing and luxury items with the remainder. As people in middle- and low-income countries become wealthier on average, they will have increased disposable income which will drive expanding markets for life-enhancing goods and services.

Rising consumption creates environmental risk
and business opportunities for innovation

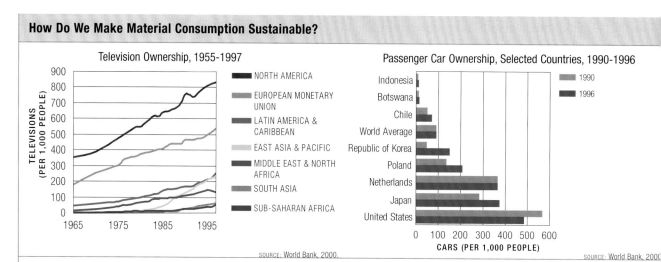

How Do We Make Material Consumption Sustainable?

Television Ownership, 1955-1997

Passenger Car Ownership, Selected Countries, 1990-1996

SOURCE: World Bank, 2000.

SOURCE: World Bank, 2000

Television ownership has soared in many parts of the developing world, and TV is a gateway to entertainment and to political, public, and commercial information and knowledge. The world's newly affluent also aspire to greater mobility (see **Mobility**). As emerging economies repeat the historical development patterns of the industrialized countries, rising car ownership and air travel will have major impacts on material consumption, land use, pollution, greenhouse gas emissions, and petroleum demand.

Facts

- The money spent on household consumption (all goods and services except real estate) worldwide increased 68% between 1980 and 1998.[1]

- Consumers in high-income countries spent $15.4 trillion of the $19.3 trillion in total private consumption in 1998. Purchases by consumers in low-income nations represented less than 4% of all private consumption.[2]

- Consumption of meat and milk in developing countries will grow between 2.8% and 3.3% per year respectively, from 1993 to 2020.[3]

- Television ownership increased five-fold in the East Asia and Pacific region from 1985-1997.[4]

- 200 million vehicles would be added to the global fleet if car ownership in China, India, and Indonesia were the same as the world average of 90 per 1,000; roughly double the number of automobiles today in the United States.[5]

- Paper consumption is rising fastest in the developing world, but the average American still consumes about 17 times more paper per year than the average citizen of the developing world.[6]

RELATED TRENDS	
Population	10
Efficiency	28
Mobility	42

The money spent on household consumption worldwide increased 68% between 1980 and 1998.

More Wealth, More Protein

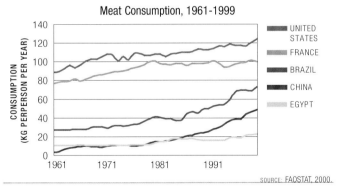

Meat Consumption, 1961-1999

Y-axis: CONSUMPTION (KG PER PERSON PER YEAR), 0 to 140
X-axis: 1961, 1971, 1981, 1991

Legend:
- UNITED STATES
- FRANCE
- BRAZIL
- CHINA
- EGYPT

SOURCE: FAOSTAT, 2000.

Consumers in developing countries quickly add more protein to their diets as their incomes rise; per capita meat consumption has exploded in the fast expanding economies of China and Brazil. Meat consumption nearly tripled in Brazil and grew 13-fold in China since 1961, though consumption in both countries is still well below that in North America and Western Europe.[7] Protein-rich diets of meat and fish, however, demand large areas of land to produce animal feed, add pollution to waterways, can erode grazing lands, and lead to over-fishing (see **Agriculture**).

Implications for Business

The world population is poised to expand 50% by 2050 and with it will come an extraordinary growth in consumption. In the past, society has met demand by increasing our extraction and harvesting efficiency and by developing substitutes. Never has there been such an opportunity and imperative for innovation that meets the needs of many new consumers without damaging the planet's natural resource base. Far-sighted companies are making resources — energy, minerals, water, timber — stretch many times further through production efficiency, development of renewable and recyclable goods, and other changes that pay for themselves and help the environment. Some consumers in the developed world are favoring companies and products they perceive as socially and environmentally responsible. New ideas are emerging to reduce impacts of consumption, such as producing zero emission vehicles, changing annual crops to perennials, creating zero waste textile mills, and utilizing electronic paper and compostable footwear. It is this kind of "radical" or "discontinuous" invention rather than incremental improvement that is the source of significant — not incremental — improvements in competitive position and shareholder value.

Since the Industrial Revolution, development and economic expansion have been tied to increased energy use. The link remains strong today — energy use is rising worldwide. Fossil fuels dominate the world's energy supply, yet the resulting greenhouse gas emissions are driving temperature changes and escalating the risks of climate change. Climate models predict that floods, droughts, and severe storms are likely to become both more frequent and more severe, costing lives, agricultural harvests, and economic progress.[1] The challenge for the energy sector is to supply electricity and services more efficiently and with less environmental impact. This challenge is especially great in the emerging economies, where energy needs are growing but disposable income and access to power grids are low. Currently, about two billion people live off the electrical generation and power grid.[2] This represents a huge market for dispersed energy systems such as photovoltaic generators, small wind turbines, hydrogen fuel cells, and biomass generators that meet rural power needs without the infrastructure of power grids, pipelines, and power plants. The market potential within the energy-hungry industrial economies for cleaner energy sources is seen in the rapid growth of wind, solar, and natural gas power.

Escalating demand for energy propels economic development
but threatens Earth's climate.

Energy Use Is Increasing Rapidly

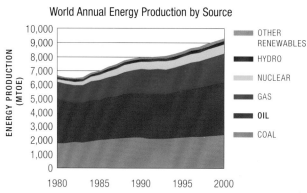

World Annual Energy Production by Source

ENERGY PRODUCTION (MTOE)

OTHER RENEWABLES
HYDRO
NUCLEAR
GAS
OIL
COAL

SOURCE: IEA, 1999 and 2000.

Three Scenarios of Global Energy Consumption Projected to 2050

FINAL ENERGY CONSUMPTION (MTOE)

CASE A: HIGH GROWTH
CASE B: MIDDLE COURS[E]
CASE C: ECOLOGICALL[Y] DRIVEN

SOURCE: IIASA/WEC, 199[?]

World energy production rose from 6,600 to 9,352 Mtoe (million tonnes of oil equivalent) — a 42% increase — between 1980 and 2000. Fossil fuels (oil, coal, and gas) account for almost all the growth and growth would have been even higher if not for energy efficiency gains made by some countries, such as China and the United States (see **Efficiency**).[3]

Across three economic growth and technological improvement scenario[s] projected energy consumption increases between 1.5-2.3 time[s] between 2000 and 2050.[4] The projected energy consumption varies [by] region, with particularly high rates of growth in the large emergin[g] economies (see **Mobility**).

Facts

Biomass contributes approximately 15% of energy supply worldwide and accounts for one fifth to one third of energy consumption in developing countries.[5]

The 1990s were the warmest decade and 1998 the warmest year on record.[6]

Wind turbines now generate over 17,000 megawatts (MW) of electricity in more than 30 countries, making wind power the world's fastest growing source of energy.[7]

Worldwide shipments of photovoltaic cells grew six-fold from 48 MW in 1990 to 288 MW in 2000; module prices (US$ per Watt) declined from US$30 to less than US$5 from 1975 to 1995 and have remained constant as the market has grown 30% per year in recent years.[8]

A Warming World

Atmospheric CO2 Concentrations, 1750-2000

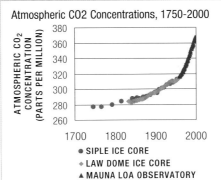

- ● SIPLE ICE CORE
- ◆ LAW DOME ICE CORE
- ▲ MAUNA LOA OBSERVATORY

Global Surface Air Temperature, 5 Year Mean, 1880-2000

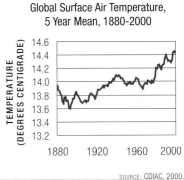

SOURCE: CDIAC, 2000.

Burning fossil fuel causes air pollutants such as sulfur and nitrogen oxides, ozone, mercury, particulate matter, and carbon dioxide (see **Pollution**). Unlike many pollutants that are short-lived in the atmosphere, greenhouse gases such as CO_2 accumulate in the atmosphere. The CO_2 concentration in the atmosphere is now nearly 370 parts per million and rising fast, up from a pre-industrial level of 288 ppm. Scientists have confirmed that global warming is occurring and is human-induced — largely the result of greenhouse gas emissions from burning fossil fuels and deforestation.[9]

World energy production rose 42% between 1980 and 2000 and will grow 150-230% by 2050.

Tomorrow's Energy Markets

Global Solar and Wind Energy Production, 1980-1997

- ▓ SOLAR
- ▓ WIND

SOURCE: IEA, 1999.

Currently, renewable energy sources (geothermal, solar, wind, and biomass) contribute approximately 11.5% of the world's energy consumption and nearly 14% if hydropower is included.[10] However, hydropower bears its own costs of damage to freshwater ecosystems and contribution to greenhouse gas emissions. "New" renewable energy sources with lower environmental impacts, like solar, wind, and geothermal are growing more quickly on a percentage basis than any other energy sources.[11] Wind power has grown from nearly zero production in the 1980s to almost one Mtoe in 1997 with a drop in price per kilowatt-hours to levels competitive with conventional energy sources.[12]

Implications for Business

Energy use meets a basic human need, but the environmental impacts of rising energy production and consumption are introducing considerable uncertainty to industries — from oil and gas to reinsurance and agriculture. These uncertainties result from the costs and benefits of climate change mitigation markets as well as from the impacts of climate change. The price of fossil fuels may rise as the market internalizes environmental externalities. In response, proactive businesses are conducting inventories of their operations to reduce energy intensity and greenhouse gas emissions.[13] Some major multinational companies have made voluntary commitments to reduce greenhouse gas emissions and to support markets for trading carbon emission allowances and reduction credits.[14] These commitments are driving new markets in alternative energies, energy conservation services, and energy efficient technologies.

W aste and pollution including emissions from fossil fuel use, persistent chemical contaminants, and waste products of economic activities are, for the most part, increasing. Evidence from developed countries and the limited data from developing countries reveal a growing waste stream of rising emissions and pollution despite successes that demonstrate the cost effectiveness of pollution avoidance and reduction measures for certain pollutants (see **Energy**).[1] Climate change, acid deposition, species extinction, public health problems, and coastal dead-zones all point to waste accumulating at rates beyond Earth's absorptive capacity. Today's economies act as a linear system: materials and energy are taken from the natural environment, put to a brief useful life, and then become waste in the atmosphere, on land, or in water.

Transport And Industry Accounts For A Large Percentage Of Air Pollutants

Emissions Sources for Selected Air Pollutants in OECD Regions, 1997

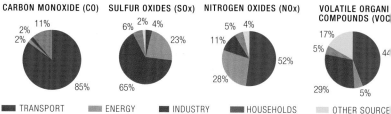

CARBON MONOXIDE (CO): 85%, 11%, 2%, 2%

SULFUR OXIDES (SOx): 65%, 23%, 4%, 2%, 6%

NITROGEN OXIDES (NOx): 52%, 28%, 11%, 5%, 4%

VOLATILE ORGANIC COMPOUNDS (VOC): 29%, 17%, 5%, 5%, 44%

■ TRANSPORT   ▨ ENERGY   ■ INDUSTRY   ■ HOUSEHOLDS   ▨ OTHER SOURCE

© OECD, 200

Pollution and waste are caused by all sectors of society but transportation (see **Mobility**) and the industrial and energy sectors play a large role in producing — and therefore ca play a large role in avoiding — some forms of pollution. Fossil fuels power our economie: 50-90% of the mass of industrialized-country outputs into the environment goes up into th atmosphere (see **Consumption**).[2]

Pollution remains
a global challenge.

Facts

- In the early 1990s, 400 million tons of hazardous waste were produced annually, about 75% of this from OECD countries, mainly from chemical production, energy production, mining, pulp and paper industry, and leather industries.[3]

- Pollution abatement and control expenditures in the United States ranged from 1.7-1.8% of GDP from the mid-1970s to the mid-1990s and totaled US$122 billion in 1994.[4]

- Estimates are that 2-6% percent of the total burden of disease in OECD countries is a result of environmental degradation — mainly from urban air quality problems, and chemicals in the environment.[5]

- Environment-related health costs in OECD countries is estimated to be between US$50-$130 billion.[6]

High Levels Of Pollution Endanger Human Health

Concentration of Key Pollutants in Major Cities, 1995-1999

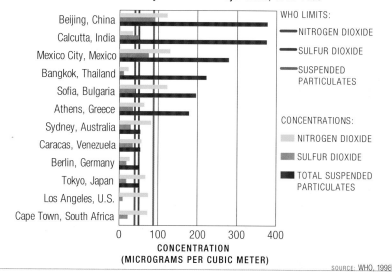

WHO LIMITS:
— NITROGEN DIOXIDE
— SULFUR DIOXIDE
— SUSPENDED PARTICULATES

CONCENTRATIONS:
▨ NITROGEN DIOXIDE
▨ SULFUR DIOXIDE
■ TOTAL SUSPENDED PARTICULATES

Cities (top to bottom): Beijing, China; Calcutta, India; Mexico City, Mexico; Bangkok, Thailand; Sofia, Bulgaria; Athens, Greece; Sydney, Australia; Caracas, Venezuela; Berlin, Germany; Tokyo, Japan; Los Angeles, U.S.; Cape Town, South Africa

CONCENTRATION (MICROGRAMS PER CUBIC METER): 0, 100, 200, 300, 400

SOURCE: WHO, 1998

Pollution takes a large toll on human and ecosystem health. In many cities, levels of SO_2, NO_2, and suspended particulates exceed healthy limits recommended by the World Health Organization (WHO). Air pollution, mostly from burning fossil fuels, causes an estimated 500,000 deaths each year and an estimated four to five million new cases of chronic bronchitis. The economic burden of this pollution is estimated at 0.5-2.5% of world GNP, about $150-$750 billion per year.[7]

Air Pollution: Going Down And Going Up

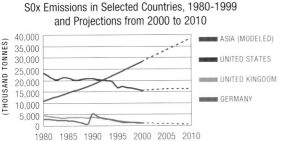

SOx Emissions in Selected Countries, 1980-1999 and Projections from 2000 to 2010

- ASIA (MODELED)
- UNITED STATES
- UNITED KINGDOM
- GERMANY

SOURCE: EMEP, 2000; McDonald, 1999.

Trends in pollution and emissions, such as sulfur oxide (SOx) emissions, often show two opposite directions in the developed vs. developing worlds. SOx pollution in many Western European nations has dropped by 75% or more since 1980, and decreased by about one quarter in the United States.[8] Asia's sulfur emissions (excluding the former Soviet Republics) are expected to rise from 18 to 48 million tonnes between 1990 and 2020 (see **Energy**).[9] Acid rain, from SOx and other acidifying emissions from fossil fuels, can severely impact agriculture and natural habitats.

Reporting And Accountability Mechanisms Can Work

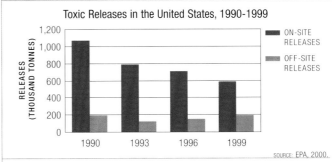

Toxic Releases in the United States, 1990-1999

- ON-SITE RELEASES
- OFF-SITE RELEASES

SOURCE: EPA, 2000.

Liability laws and the public reporting of toxic releases in the United States, and similar mechanisms in other OECD countries indicate that disclosure laws can lead to reductions in toxic releases. Toxic releases from industries tracked since 1987 by the United States Toxic Release Inventory (TRI) have dropped by nearly half (see **Accountability**). Toxic release data from industries newly followed since 1998 indicate that toxic releases are not uniformly decreasing and threaten to continue creating a dangerous and expensive toxic legacy.[10] The total cost to remediate contaminated sites in 13 OECD countries has been estimated to be about US$330 billion.[11]

RELATED TRENDS	
Accountability	52
Urbanization	40
Health	16

50-90% of the mass
of industrialized-country environment outflows
goes up into the atmosphere.

The CFC Success Story

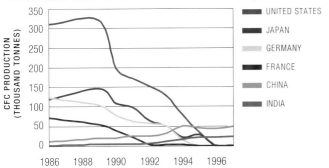

Production of Chlorofluorocarbons in Selected Countries, 1986-1997

- UNITED STATES
- JAPAN
- GERMANY
- FRANCE
- CHINA
- INDIA

SOURCE: UNEP, 1999.

Concerted efforts to reduce industrial pollution have been successful when backed by industry and governments such as in the cases of SO₂ and chlorofluorocarbons (CFCs). The production of CFCs was reduced dramatically by most countries between 1986–1996.[12] Efforts to repeat this success with persistent organic pollutants (POPs) — associated with acute environmental toxicity, human reproductive disorders, birth defects, and cancer — are underway.[13]

Implications for Business

Polluting emissions of most types are rising worldwide and improvements in the developed world may be overshadowed by the waste from industrialization and consumption in the developing world. Waste and emissions represent lost value, business costs, and a threat to present and future human generations and to ecosystem health. Harmonization of business operations to a single high standard, international regulations, legal mechanisms for accountability, and civil society action are likely to further inflate the costs of waste management and to raise the risk of pollution-related financial and reputational liabilities. Innovation to avoid waste, use renewable resources, and develop industrial models in which wastes are captured and treated as an input into other processes can reduce costs and increase revenues. Examples of approaches that can reduce emissions and waste are renewable energy sources, transition from fossil fuel-based materials to raw materials from renewable and biodegradable sources, and industrial complexes that re-use waste heat, materials, and water.

E conomic growth at both the company and national economy level has historically been linked to increased resource use and waste production, but many businesses and economies have recently demonstrated that improving efficiency can break this link. Greater efficiency is achieved via process improvements, waste and product recycling, less material-intensive product designs, remanufacturing, and other approaches, delivering benefits for competitiveness and the bottom line. Despite efficiency gains and unlinking economic growth from total material use, waste production is still rising across the globe. Developing nations tend to use less material and generate less waste per capita than more developed countries, yet employ materials less efficiently and, like developed countries, are increasing their total material use. Policy changes, economic gains from improved efficiency, consumer preference for eco-friendly products, and advocacy are all driving improvements in the efficiency of businesses and economies. Continued movement toward an efficient and sustainable economy will require a cyclical production model in which materials previously discarded as waste are captured and used as resources.

Throughput still grows even as energy and materials efficiency improves

Facts

- The United States recycles about 65% of its steel.[1]

- In 2000, European primary aluminum production was 3.8 million tonnes and recycled aluminum production was 2.25 million tonnes.[2]

- Paper recycling into paper and fiber products has risen over the past three decades to about 40% of total paper production worldwide.[3]

- In 1999, Brazil recycled 5.8 billion aluminum cans accounting for 73% of national can production and supporting a US$55 million industry.[4]

Entire Economies Are Improving Efficiency

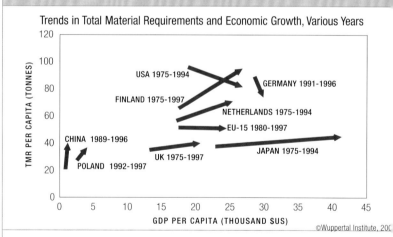

Trends in Total Material Requirements and Economic Growth, Various Years

©Wuppertal Institute, 200

Total material throughput of a nation's economy can decrease even as GDP rises.[5] In th European Union (EU), per capita total material requirements (TMR: the sum of all imported ar domestically produced material inputs into the economy) have remained stable between 198 and 1996. However, the amount of value created with that material increased significantl GDP of the EU grew 40% over the same time period. This trend is not universal; China's GD per capita grew modestly from 1989 to 1996 while its total material requirement grew by we over 50%. Other countries, such as Finland or Poland where both GDP per capita and TM grew rapidly from 1975 to 1997, saw little overall efficiency gain.[6] Between 1975–1996, th U.S. economy demonstrated decoupling between material use and economic growth, but th total burden on the environment, indicated by material outputs, still mounted.[7]

Industry Can Spearhead Efficiency Gains

Industrial Energy Use per Share of GDP in Selected Countries, 1970-1997

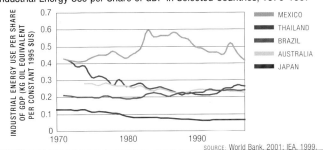

SOURCE: World Bank, 2001; IEA, 1999.

Examples of Efficiency Gains in Selected Industries

INDUSTRY	YEARS	EFFICIENCY GAIN PER UNIT OUTPUT
European Union Chemical Industry	1985 to 1996	34% Less Energy
United States Chemical Industry	1974 to 1998	43% Less Energy
European Paper Industry	1975 to 1997	50-80% Less Water
European and Canadian Paper Industry	1990 to 1998	10.5% Less Energy
Steel Industry in 10 OECD Countries	1971 to 1991	20% Less Energy

SOURCE: OECD, 2001.

Industrial energy efficiency is improving in many countries around the world. The amount of energy needed by the industrial sector to generate income has fallen over time with specific industries making tremendous strides in improving efficiency. For example, the U.S. chemical industry reduced energy consumption by 43% per unit of production since 1975, and the European paper industry shrank water usage by 50% to 80% per unit of production (see **Water**).[8]

Paper recycling into paper and fiber products has risen over the past three decades to about 40% of total paper production worldwide.

RELATED TRENDS

Energy	24
Water	36
Communications	44

Promising Markets For Recycling And Efficient Products

Total Paper Production and Recovered Paper Production, 1970-2000

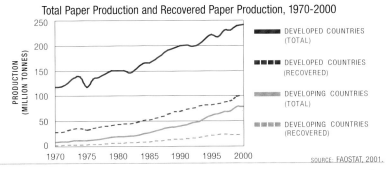

SOURCE: FAOSTAT, 2001.

Part of the observed decline in the waste intensity of economic activity is due to capturing materials for reuse.[9] Recycling of paper has kept pace or grown faster than paper production in the developed and developing worlds. The 40% of total worldwide paper production recovered for recycling into fiber-based products includes both consumer and production process wastes.[10] Efficiency gains over the life-cycle of product manufacturing are made from capturing waste materials and heat for reuse, sale, or trade. Consumer demand, activism, and regulations drive markets for energy efficient products. Light bulbs, washing machines, air conditioners, refrigerators, and other household appliances are being improved to provide the same services while using less energy. For example, reduced price, improved performance, electricity costs, and environmental awareness have propelled an almost 10-fold increase in the worldwide sales of compact fluorescent lamps (CFLs) in the last decade.[11] Other trends are less positive, such as the large investments in the development and marketing of sport utility vehicles in the United States and other countries (see **Consumption**).

Implications for Business

The last decade of growth in many countries has proven that value can rise while material and energy throughput decreases. But while overall industrial efficiency is improving, total materials throughput and waste generation continue to grow. Efficiency enhances competitiveness and reduces environmental liability. As efficiency is sought by businesses and imposed by regulations on both production and consumption, competitive advantage will accrue to those who serve the market demand for efficient products. Improving efficiency promises continued returns for industry; the transfer of eco-efficient technologies and practices to growing economies is both a growth market in itself and a means to earn license-to-operate in new markets. Successful companies in this century will focus on production processes and business models that recycle raw materials, process outputs and finished products through the value chain and the product life cycle.

Natural Capital

- Ecosystems
- Agriculture
- Freshwater

PRESERVING THE RESOURCE BASE

The world economy depends on a base of natural resources — our "natural capital" — that is showing signs of severe degradation. Without improved environmental performance, future business operations will be exposed to risks of rising prices for water, materials, and for waste disposal. Those businesses that reduce the environmental impacts of their operations, goods, and services will win competitive advantages. Protecting the long-term license-to-operate in existing and new markets depends on business strategies that preserve and renew natural habitats and critical environmental resources.

Ecosystems — communities of species that interact with each other and the physical settings in which they live — represent capital in the portfolio of natural assets that yields our livelihoods and supports our well-being. Ecosystems such as grasslands, forests, coastal areas, and rivers supply food, water, air, biodiversity, climate stability, provide places for aesthetic enjoyment and recreation, and process our wastes. They provide jobs and income: in the 1990s, agriculture, forestry, and fishing accounted for approximately four of every ten jobs worldwide, five of ten jobs in East Asian and Pacific countries, and six of ten jobs in Sub-Saharan Africa.[1] In a quarter of the world's nations, crops, timber, and fish still contribute more to the economy than industrial goods. Declining agricultural productivity, diminished supplies of freshwater, reduced timber yields, and declining fish harvests have taken a significant toll on many local economies.

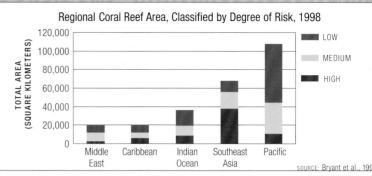

Coral Reef Destruction Undermines Coastal Economies

Regional Coral Reef Area, Classified by Degree of Risk, 1998

SOURCE: Bryant et al., 199

Approximately 150,000 square kilometers of coral reefs worldwide are at medium high levels of risk of degradation; the threat is greatest in Southeast Asia and the Pacif regions. Direct human activities such as over-fishing, destructive fishing, and polluti and sedimentation from human settlement, deforestation, industry, and agriculture a the greatest immediate threats.[2] "Coral bleaching" is a common coral killer and may b one of the first clear impacts of climate change on biodiversity.[3] Degradation of cor ecosystems and the resulting loss of fish habitat and the decline in tourism jeopardiz the livelihoods of some coastal communities and tourism-dependent island nations.[4]

The productive capacity of the planet is in decline.

Facts

- Nearly 26,000 plant species — about 10% of all known plant species — are under threat of extinction.[5] More than 1,100 mammals and 1,200 birds, 700 freshwater fish, and hundreds of reptiles and amphibians are also threatened with extinction.[6]

- Invasive species are a worldwide problem, e.g., non-native trees in South Africa's Western Cape use more water than native species and threaten to cut Cape Town's water supply by about one third in the next century.[7]

- The United States has lost an estimated 53% of its wetlands.[8] Current repair of the natural functions of the Florida Everglades to restore habitat, water provision, and flood control is estimated to cost US$7.8 billion.[9]

- In 1997, the global market for natural-product derived pharmaceuticals was estimated at US$75-$120 billion.[10]

- Human-induced evolution (acquisition of resistance) in some major pests and pathogens approaches a US$50 billion cost to the United States economy and probably exceeds US$100 billion.[11]

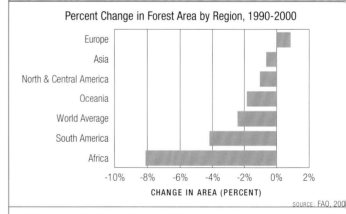

Forest Loss Impacts Clean Water, Biodiversity, And Climate

Percent Change in Forest Area by Region, 1990-2000

CHANGE IN AREA (PERCENT)

SOURCE: FAO, 200

Between 1990 and 2000, Africa and South America — the regions of some o the world's largest surviving tropical forests — lost 8% and 4% of their tot forests, respectively.[12] The world lost a net average of 2% of its forests durin that decade.[13] These percentages represent huge areas: 16.1 million hectare of forest were lost per year to deforestation and conversion to plantatior during the 1990s, 94% of this in the tropics.[14] Forests act as water reservoir and filters, provide home and livelihoods for human populations, and play a important stabilizing role for Earth's climate (see **Freshwater**). Approximate 35–40% of Earth's carbon is stored in forests, and land use change (principal deforestation) releases roughly 20% of all annual carbon emissions.[15]

Are Fleets Exploiting Marine Resources Past The Point Of Recovery?

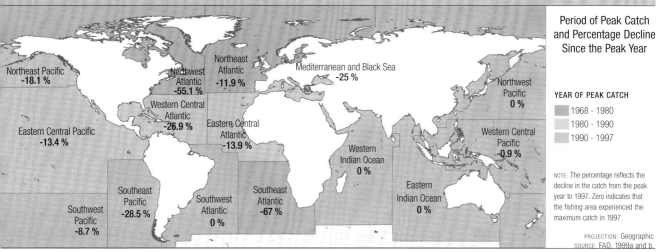

Period of Peak Catch and Percentage Decline Since the Peak Year

Northeast Pacific -18.1 %

Northwest Atlantic -55.1 %

Northeast Atlantic -11.9 %

Mediterranean and Black Sea -25 %

Northwest Pacific 0 %

Western Central Atlantic -26.9 %

Eastern Central Pacific -13.4 %

Eastern Central Atlantic -13.9 %

Western Indian Ocean 0 %

Western Central Pacific -0.9 %

Southeast Pacific -28.5 %

Southwest Atlantic 0 %

Southeast Atlantic -67 %

Eastern Indian Ocean 0 %

Southwest Pacific -8.7 %

YEAR OF PEAK CATCH
- 1968 - 1980
- 1980 - 1990
- 1990 - 1997

NOTE: The percentage reflects the decline in the catch from the peak year to 1997. Zero indicates that the fishing area experienced the maximum catch in 1997.

PROJECTION: Geographic
SOURCE: FAO, 1999a and b.

Fisheries are a major international industry: total fisheries catch in 1997 was valued at US$81 billion.[16] However, marine fisheries are showing signs of strain from over-exploitation. The last 20 years have seen great geographic expansion by industrial fleets, intensified fishing, and improved technology but total fisheries catch has remained relatively constant since the mid-1980s.[17] Larger fishing fleets have had to continuously move to less-exploited fish species and less-exploited regions as they progressively harvest areas beyond their capacity to recover (see **Agriculture**).

Nearly 26,000 plant species, more than 1,100 mammals and 1,200 birds, 700 freshwater fish, and hundreds of reptiles and amphibians are threatened with extinction.

RELATED TRENDS	
Energy	24
Population	10
Emissions	26

Ecosystem Stewardship Creates New Market Opportunities

Certified Forest Area by Region, 2000

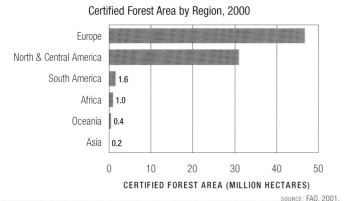

Region	
Europe	
North & Central America	
South America	1.6
Africa	1.0
Oceania	0.4
Asia	0.2

CERTIFIED FOREST AREA (MILLION HECTARES)

SOURCE: FAO, 2001.

Regulatory pressures, social activism, and consumer preferences are driving producers and retailers to offer a range of products — timber, coffee, fruits and vegetables, wine and others — that are certified as produced in an environmentally and/or socially responsible manner (see **Agriculture**). About 2% of forests worldwide are certified as managed for sustainable yield and for provision of wildlife habitat, clean water, biodiversity, and other ecological services.[18] While the percentage of the total markets filled by certified products is now small, growth rates are very high.

Implications for Business

The private sector has an interest — and an economic opportunity — in managing the natural capital portfolio wisely. Many of the goods and services supplied by ecosystems cannot be replaced at any reasonable price. There is a growing interest in treating ecosystem goods and services not as "free" common goods, but as assets with a market value in order to provide incentive for their conservation. Economies are developing for the goods and services that ecosystems supply through creation of new property rights, markets for CO_2 emissions credits, markets for sustainable agriculture products, water pricing schemes, and other incentive systems. As these markets emerge, competitive advantage will go to businesses that can reduce environmental impacts, embody environmental performance in consumer products, innovate services that protect and renew the environment, and that reduce the costs and liabilities associated with ecosystem damage.

Agriculture

How we choose to produce food may determine the future of grasslands, forests, marine ecosystems, and other ecosystems. Keeping pace with population growth and alleviating existing malnutrition over the next decades will require greater food production with less environmental impact (see **Nutrition**). There are many warning signs that the agricultural system is under stress. Soil erosion, reductions in rates of cereal yield gains, plunging fish stocks, and contamination of waterways are widespread problems. Land clearing for agricultural production to support grain and animal protein demand has degraded or destroyed forests and grasslands. The world harvest of grains, livestock, and fish employs more water, labor, and land than any other human activity, making ecologically effective food production one of the primary goals of both economic and human development.

Facts

- About 30% of the potential area of temperate, subtropical, and tropical forests and about 40% of temperate grasslands (grasslands, savannas, and shrublands) have been converted to agriculture.[1]

- Cropland and managed pastures cover approximately 28% of planetary land surface, of which 31% is crops and 69% is pasture.[2]

- In 1997, food production was valued at about US$1.3 trillion per year and employed about 1.3 billion people.[3]

- Dams built for irrigation and energy generation fragment rivers and destroy wetland and aquatic habitats. There were 5,750 large dams (>15 meters high) in 1950; today there are over 45,000.[4]

- World consumption of meat has more than tripled in the past four decades, outpacing population growth and exceeding 225 million metric tons per year; 37% of all grain consumption is for animal feed

Food production is the basis of many economies but threatens the ecosystems upon which it depends.

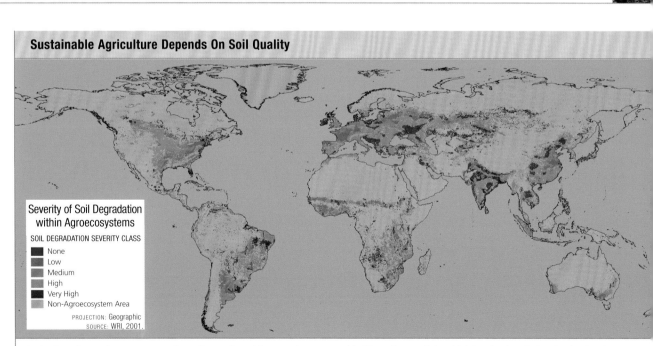

Sustainable Agriculture Depends On Soil Quality

Severity of Soil Degradation within Agroecosystems

SOIL DEGRADATION SEVERITY CLASS

- None
- Low
- Medium
- High
- Very High
- Non-Agroecosystem Area

PROJECTION: Geographic
SOURCE: WRI, 2001.

Agriculture is a primary source of employment and income for many developing countries and generates over one third of GDP in many low-income countries.[6] Agricultural crops can be very valuable, particularly in densely settled areas in China, Southeast Asia, and Europe, but also in parts of Africa and South America where export crops are grown. Half or more of the labor force in East, South and Southeast Asia, and Sub-Saharan Africa is directly involved in agriculture (see **Labor**).

Healthy soils are vital to high levels of agricultural value but large areas of productive land have been degraded by human mismanagement and climatic effects. Degradation of agricultural land (such as erosion, salinization, water-logging, nutrient depletion, acidification, and pollution) endangers food production and livelihoods. Worldwide, more than 40% of agricultural land is moderately degraded, 9% is strongly degraded and degradation has reduced worldwide crop productivity by approximately 13%.[7]

Reliance On Inputs Is Rising

Nitrogenous Fertilizer Consumption, 1975-1999

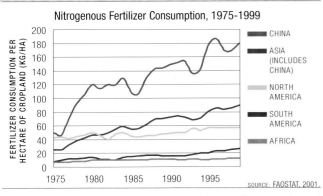

SOURCE: FAOSTAT, 2001.

Nitrogen fertilizers and irrigation are being used more and more to raise and maintain crop yields as farmers gain access to advanced production inputs (see **Freshwater**). This is particularly apparent in the fast growth and high rates of fertilizer use in China. Stagnant yields in Africa are partly due to the many African farmers who do not have access to or cannot afford effective irrigation and fertilizer. However, water drainage from high application rates of nitrogen fertilizers can lead to dead zones in rivers, lakes, and coasts.

Concerned Consumers Create Hot Markets

Organic Retail Sales, Forecast for 2000 ($US Millions)

SOURCE: Willer and Yussefi, 2001.

Certification standards are spreading worldwide for "organic" food — food produced without chemical inputs and to various standards of ecosystem stewardship. Today's worldwide retail market of US$20 billion for organic-certified products is growing approximately 10% to 30% annually in the industrial nations.[8] More than 130 countries produce certified organic food in commercial quantities including at least 65 developing countries.[9]

> About 30% of the potential area of temperate, subtropical, and tropical forests and about 40% of temperate grasslands have been converted to agriculture.

RELATED TRENDS

Farmed Fish Becomes Big Business

Aquaculture Production and Total Marine and Freshwater Fish Harvest, 1980-1999

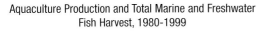
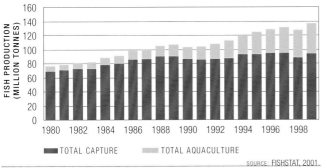

SOURCE: FISHSTAT, 2001.

Rising demand and declining productivity of marine and freshwater ecosystems have driven the modernization and fast growth of aquaculture (see **Ecosystems**). Farmed fish and shellfish production has grown in volume more than tenfold since 1970, rising from 3.5 million to 42.8 million metric tons and in value from US$12 billion in 1984 to US$53.5 billion in 1999.[10] Aquaculture solves some problems of over-fishing but can create high environmental costs in coastal land use, water pollution, and use of ocean-caught fish in fish feeds.

Implications for Business

The success of the past half century at meeting world food needs has been matched by the continued degradation of the productive capacity of natural systems. The concept of sustainability has been described as living off of the interest of natural capital without harming the principal. The greatest threats to ecosystems are the conversion of land and water habitats for agricultural uses or their destruction by over-harvesting; how we produce human food, animal feed, and fiber will largely determine the preservation of biodiversity and ecosystems. The private sector plays an important role by supporting agricultural research, transferring knowledge, products, and agricultural practices with which farmers can conserve and protect resources such as water, soil, and plant and animal species. New approaches — from organic farming, to fish-farming, to genetic engineering — are transforming how we produce and conceive of food and also impact our capacity to protect and restore vital natural resources.

Water availability is arguably the world's most pressing resource issue. Water is essential for all living things, has shaped human societies for millennia, and is the basis of business activities such as cooling, food processing, chemical synthesis, and irrigation. Growing water scarcity and alarming declines in aquatic biodiversity are evidence that water policies and practices in most parts of the world are failing to protect life's most vital resource. Population growth, industrialization, urbanization, agricultural intensification, and water-intensive lifestyles are placing great stress on freshwater systems, with both water use and pollution driving the scarcity of useable water. Surfacewater quality has improved in most developed countries during the past 20 years, though nitrate and pesticide contamination remain persistent problems. Data on water quality in other regions of the world are sparse, but water quality appears to be compromised in almost all regions and continues to decline in areas with intense agricultural development and rapid urbanization.

Facts

- Over the past century, world water withdrawals increased almost twice as fast as population growth.[1]

- More than 20% of the world's 10,000 recorded freshwater fish species have become extinct, threatened, or endangered in recent decades.[2] Factors contributing to freshwater fish extinction include habitat alterations (71%), non-native species (54%), overfishing (29%), and pollution (26%).[3]

- In 60% of the European cities with more than 100,000 people, groundwater is being used at a faster rate than it can be replenished.[4] Cities that have experienced aquifer drops between 10 to 50 meters include Mexico City, Bangkok, Manila, Beijing, Madras, and Shanghai.[5]

- Water pricing is a clear trend in developed countries; 17 of 18 OECD countries surveyed showed annual increases in household water prices in the 1990s.[6]

Freshwater is growing scarce amidst competing human needs

Thirsty Crops Dominate World Water Withdrawal

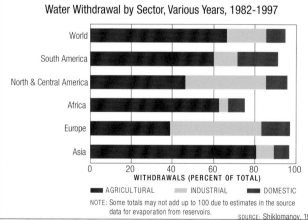

Water Withdrawal by Sector, Various Years, 1982-1997

AGRICULTURAL   INDUSTRIAL   DOMESTIC

NOTE: Some totals may not add up to 100 due to estimates in the source data for evaporation from reservoirs.
SOURCE: Shiklomanov, 1997.

Irrigated Cropland as a Percent of Total Cropland, 1961-1997

SOURCE: World Bank, 2000

Seventy percent of all freshwater withdrawal is for agriculture.[7] Inefficiency abounds in water usage and exacerbates scarcity problems; over half of the water withdrawn for irrigation never reaches the target crop because of leakage and evaporation.[8] Overuse of agricultural inputs such as chemical fertilizers, pesticides, and manure contaminates water supplies with nutrients like nitrates, phosphorus, and heavy metals that can cause significant problems for water quality (see **Agriculture**).[9]

40% Of The World Will Live In Water-Scarce Regions By 2025

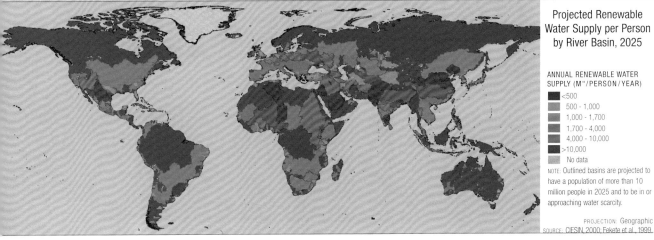

Projected Renewable Water Supply per Person by River Basin, 2025

ANNUAL RENEWABLE WATER SUPPLY (M"/PERSON/YEAR)
- ■ <500
- 500 - 1,000
- 1,000 - 1,700
- 1,700 - 4,000
- 4,000 - 10,000
- ■ >10,000
- No data

NOTE: Outlined basins are projected to have a population of more than 10 million people in 2025 and to be in or approaching water scarcity.

PROJECTION: Geographic
SOURCE: CIESIN, 2000; Fekete et al., 1999.

Large areas of the world experience "water stress," defined as below 1,700 cubic meters per year per person.[10] In areas where supplies drop below 1,000 cubic meters per person, shortages disrupt both food production and economic development unless the region is wealthy enough to apply new technologies for water conservation and re-use. An estimated 2.3 billion people, 41% of the world's population, currently live in water-stressed areas. By 2025, 3.5 billion are projected to live in water-stressed areas.[11] Water scarcity has also led to conflict between upstream and downstream areas within countries, and tense relations between countries sharing a transnational waterway or watershed.[12]

Over the past century, world water withdrawals increased almost twice as fast as population growth.

RELATED TRENDS

Health	16
Efficiency	28
Privatization	54

Access To Safe Water Improves But Still Eludes Many

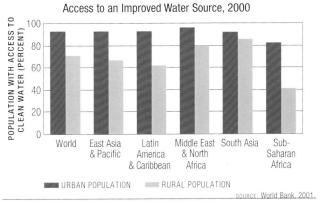

Access to an Improved Water Source, 2000

POPULATION WITH ACCESS TO CLEAN WATER (PERCENT)

World — East Asia & Pacific — Latin America & Caribbean — Middle East & North Africa — South Asia — Sub-Saharan Africa

■ URBAN POPULATION   RURAL POPULATION

SOURCE: World Bank, 2001.

Over one billion people worldwide, most in rural areas, lack access to a safe water source and more than 2.5 billion people do not have access to adequate sanitation facilities.[13] Unclean water and poor hygiene take an enormous toll on the health of populations through preventable disease; there are approximately 1.5 billion cases annually of diarrhea in children under the age of 5, resulting in 3.3 million deaths (see **Health**).[14] Trachoma, a water-borne bacteria, caused blindness in 6 million people, and water-borne parasites led to 700 million cases of hookworm and 1.3 billion cases of roundworm.[15]

Implications for Business

The pressures on freshwater supplies portend rising water costs and an urgent need to improve water-use efficiency. Short water supplies will make it difficult for water-intensive businesses to site their activities in arid regions and will increase water-related costs everywhere. Raising prices for water usage can send signals to consumers that conservation is good for the environment as well as to investors to attract funding for essential water infrastructure. True cost recovery for water is made difficult by subsidies that include public investment in irrigation projects, irrigation water pricing, urban and industrial infrastructure, and uncompensated environmental damage from water over-use and pollution. Increases in industrial water efficiency as well as private sector involvement in water management hold promise; reduction of water use, closed-loop systems, and elimination of water discharges can lower water costs, energy costs for pumping and cooling, and wastewater treatment costs. Water scarcity may create a new arena for business differentiation — those with water-efficient processes or products may have greater operational flexibility and more competitive cost structures in a water-stressed world.

Connections

- ☐ **Urbanization**
- ☐ **Mobility**
- ☐ **Communications**
- ☐ **Labor**

DOING BUSINESS
IN A NETWORKED WORLD

We live in a world of rapid change and a
growing density of human and technological
networks. People are concentrating in cities
with greater access to information and
transportation networks. Information and
knowledge propagate at light speed, and
people and goods move around the globe
as never before. In this integrated world,
businesses have a crucial stake in economic
development, healthy cities, efficient and
accessible mobility, and in expanding the
pool of educated workers and consumers.

There is a steady growth of urban areas worldwide — the result of population growth within cities, rural-to-urban migration, rural ecological degradation, a workforce shift from agriculture to industry, public investment in cities rather than rural areas, and political change. People are attracted from rural areas to cities in search of jobs and greater access to education, healthcare, transportation, and markets. Numerous large cities have grown into "megacities" — metropolitan areas of more than 10 million people — though small and medium-size cities remain home to the majority of urban dwellers.[1] The current pace and scale of urban growth strains the capacity of many local and national governments to provide basic services to residents. With suitable development strategies and investment in infrastructure, urban areas in the developing world can become important and readily accessible markets; they also typically offer the private sector access to a better-educated, healthier workforce than rural areas. However, without significant investments in infrastructure, cities can become incubators for smog, crime, polluted water, disease, and slums that all jeopardize human health, productivity, and the natural resource base.

The Birth Of The 20 Million Resident "Megacity"

Percent of Total Population that is Urban, 1975-2015

MORE DEVELOPED REGIONS

WORLD

LESS DEVELOPED REGIONS

SOURCE: UN Population Division, 199

The growth in the number of megacities has been particularly strik-ing in the past several decades. In 1950, only New York had ove 10 million residents and London, Paris, Moscow, Essen, Bueno Aires and Chicago were among the ten largest cities. Today ther are 19 cities of over 10 million residents; in 2015 the number expected to be 23 and some will soon exceed 20 million people Many of the largest cities are now in Asian, African, and Lati American developing countries.[2]

Urban growth concentrates business opportunitie and societal challenges.

Facts

- By 2010, more than 50% of all people will live in urban areas. In developing countries, the proportion of urban dwellers will rise from less than 20% in 1950 to more than 40% in 2010.[3]

- Of the world's fastest growing cities with population greater than 750,000, 2% are located in high-income countries, 40% are in middle-income countries, and 60% are in low-income countries. Asia is home to 60% of these cities, Africa to 25%, and Latin America to 15%.[4]

- The current addition of 60 million new urban citizens a year is the equivalent of adding another Paris, Beijing, or Cairo every other month.[5]

- The health consequences of urban air pollution are high; each year, suspended particulate matter may account for 460,000 premature deaths, and SO_2 for 370,000 premature deaths.[6]

- Developing-nation cities often lack adequate solid waste disposal; in Northern African cities, 20-80% of solid waste is disposed of by open dumping.[7]

- Projections of municipal solid waste in Asia predict a rise from 2.7 million cubic meters (m^3) per day in 1999 to 5.2 million m^3 per day in 2025; solid waste management costs Asian cities US$25 billion per year.[8]

Living In An Urban World

World Urban Population by City Size, 1975 -2015

CITY SIZE:

- 10 MILLION OR MORE
- 5 TO 10 MILLIO
- 1 TO 5 MILLION
- 500,000 TO 1 MILLION
- FEWER THAN 500,000

SOURCE: UN Population Division, 1999

Urban growth started long ago in the developed world where about 76% of people now live in urban areas. The proportion of urban dwellers in the developing world is much lower but the growth rate in the past two decades has been very rapid (see **Wealth**). The fastest urban growth has occurred in many intermediate-size cities with populations of 1 million to 5 million which grew in number by 80% in the last 20 years.[9] These cities are as diverse as Phoenix, United States (2.6 million), Shenzhen, China (1.1 million), and Guatemala City, Guatemala (3.2 million). Many countries direct their resources to their largest urban centers, leaving smaller cities and rural areas neglected in terms of infrastructure and services.

The World's Largest Cities

Present and Future

2000	CITY	POP. (millions)
1	Tokyo, Japan	26.4
2	Mexico City, Mexico	18.1
3	Bombay, India	18.1
4	São Paulo, Brazil	17.8
5	New York, U.S.A.	16.6
6	Lagos, Nigeria	13.4
7	Los Angeles, U.S.A.	13.1
8	Calcutta, India	12.9
9	Shanghai, China	12.9
10	Buenos Aires, Argentina	12.6
TOTAL NUMBER OF MEGACITIES:	**19**	

2015	CITY	POP. (millions)
1	Tokyo, Japan	26.4
2	Bombay, India	26.1
3	Lagos, Nigeria	23.2
4	Dhaka, Bangladesh	21.1
5	São Paulo, Brazil	20.4
6	Karachi, Pakistan	19.2
7	Mexico City, Mexico	19.2
8	New York, U.S.A.	17.4
9	Jakarta, Indonesia	17.3
10	Calcutta, India	17.3
TOTAL NUMBER OF MEGACITIES:	**23**	

SOURCE: UN Population Division, 1999.

People And Their Impacts Are Crowded Into Coastal Zones

The World's Largest Urban Population Centers, Projected to 2015

● 5 million - 10 million

● Greater than 10 million

PROJECTION: Geographic
SOURCE: ESRI, 2001.

Approximately 3.2 billion people (over 50% of the world's population) live within 200 kilometers of a coast and by 2025 the proportion of coastal dwellers is expected to be more than 75%, or an estimated 6.3 billion people.[10] Growing coastal populations and large paved urban areas lead to heavier pollutant and sediment loads that impact the ability of sensitive coastal ecosystems to provide goods and services such as shoreline protection, healthy fisheries, water filtration, and sites for recreation and tourism (see **Freshwater**).

The current addition of 60 million new urban citizens a year is the equivalent of adding the urban population of Paris, Beijing, or Cairo every other month.

RELATED TRENDS

Health	16
Water	36
Privatization	54

Rural Neglect Makes Cities Attractive

Comparison of Urban-Rural Statistics, Selected Countries, 1996-2000

	INDIA Urban	Rural	VIETNAM Urban	Rural	TANZANIA Urban	Rural
Under-Five Mortality (PER 1,000 LIVE BIRTHS)	63	104	32	48	122	151
Access to Adequate Sanitation (PERCENT OF HOUSEHOLDS)	73	14	86	70	98	86
Currently Using Contraception (PERCENT OF ALL WOMEN)	58	45	79	74	29	12.4
Median Years of Schooling (MEN)	8.3	5.8	8.1	5.4	5.7	2.1

NOTE: Sanitation data is for 2000 (all countries). All other data from India is for 1998-99; from Vietnam, 1997; from Tanzania, 1996.

SOURCE: Demographic and Health Survey, 1996, 1997 and 1999; World Bank, 2001.

The examples in this table illustrate that rural residents may have good reason to migrate to urban areas. Urban residents tend to enjoy better access to drinking water, sanitation, health services, jobs, and educational opportunities than their rural counterparts. While these benefits often do not extend to the poorest groups in a city, the chances of getting access are often better than in rural areas.

Implications for Business

In the next decade, more than half of the world's population will live in urban areas. Businesses often benefit from the growth of urban areas with their demand for energy and infrastructure, and their concentration of labor and consumers. The greatest change in urban populations will occur in developing countries which will raise new challenges but also lower the costs of serving the needs of these consumers. Sustaining and capitalizing on these opportunities will require business strategies and public-private partnerships that make cities better places in which to work, to operate a business, and to live. Improved land-use planning, health services, education, and water and sanitation services are urban priorities beyond the capacity of many local governments without private sector partnership.

Humans are increasingly mobile due to growing access to roads, cars, public transport, and airplanes. Still, the majority of people walk or bike to market, work, or school and millions of tons of goods are transported on people's backs, in cattle carts, and by pushcart. Movement of people and goods is essential to economic and business development. Mobility permits the division of labor, urban growth, trade in raw materials, fast and cheap cargo trade, and the quick transfer of employees. The global flux of people diversifies the workplace and the marketplace and fosters both formal and informal channels for the exchange of knowledge and information. All this mobility creates a large demand for energy and infrastructure. Access to less polluting and more efficient mobility is both a challenge and an opportunity for business.

Humans are more mobile, accelerating the flow of goods and knowledge and raising the demand for energy and infrastructure.

Facts

- In 1997, 54% of the oil purchased by OECD countries was for transport, with 62% projected in 2020.[1]

- With little variation around the world, people spend about an hour a day in transit, although those with higher incomes travel greater distances.[2]

- Transport of people and goods is responsible for about one fifth of worldwide energy consumption. Two thirds of transport energy demand in OECD countries is from passenger travel.[3]

- Ocean shipping of cargo has nearly doubled since 1975.[4]

- Mobility of populations and of high-risk individuals such as freight truck drivers is a significant factor in the spread of HIV/AIDS in Southern and Eastern Africa.[5]

Low Cost Shipping Spurs International Markets

Ocean Shipping Demand, 1975-1995 (trillion tonne-km)

YEAR	CRUDE PETROLEUM & PETROLEUM PRODUCTS	DRY BULK CARGO	GENERAL CARGO	TOTAL	CONTAINERIZED SHARE OF GENERAL CARGO
1975	15.7	5.0	4.5	25.2	0.0%
1980	14.7	6.6	6.0	27.3	20.7%
1985	8.3	7.2	5.6	21.1	30.1%
1990	12.6	8.5	6.5	27.6	35.1%
1995	15.0	9.4	8.1	32.5	43.7%

SOURCE: WBCSD, 20

Freight transportation has been rising and consumes about 43% of transportation fuel, yet shipping often adds less than 1% to the cost of an item. Expanded use of containers, bigger ocean liners, and lower fuel costs have combined to reduce this cost of shipping and drive a global economy. Freight trade brings value to businesses and to individuals' quality of life yet also drives environmental degradation and other social problems. Freight carriers — ocean liners, trucks, airplanes, trains, and barges — contribute to water and air pollution, habitat alteration, and the movement of invasive species, and play a role in increasing urban congestion (see **Ecosystems**).[6]

Travel Is Growing Everywhere

Total Road Traffic in Selected Countries, 1999

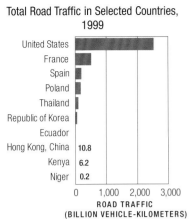

United States	
France	
Spain	
Poland	
Thailand	
Republic of Korea	
Ecuador	
Hong Kong, China	10.8
Kenya	6.2
Niger	0.2

ROAD TRAFFIC
(BILLION VEHICLE-KILOMETERS)

Increase in Road Traffic in Selected Countries, 1990-1999

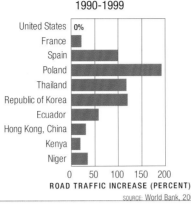

United States	0%
France	
Spain	
Poland	
Thailand	
Republic of Korea	
Ecuador	
Hong Kong, China	
Kenya	
Niger	

ROAD TRAFFIC INCREASE (PERCENT)

SOURCE: World Bank, 2001.

Global Number of Air Passengers, 1974-1998

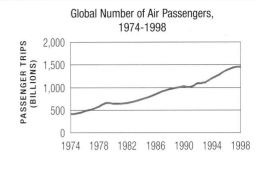

SOURCE: World Bank, 2000.

Travel by road and air has increased dramatically in recent decades while the share of travel by mass transit has decreased almost everywhere.[7] Passenger air trips have almost tripled in the last 25 years and are expected to triple again in the next 20 years.[8] The number of motor vehicles worldwide is increasing about 3% per year.[9] Rich countries have approximately 60 times more vehicles per capita than the average low-income country, but vehicle ownership has tripled in low-income countries in the past 17 years.[10] Countries like Cambodia, El Salvador, South Korea, and Thailand more than doubled the road traffic (number of vehicles multiplied by average distance they travel) within their borders between 1990 and 1999 (see **Consumption**).[11]

Transport of people and goods is responsible for about one fifth of worldwide energy consumption.

RELATED TRENDS	
Energy	24
Wealth	12
Democracy	50

Transport Drives Society's Thirst For Fuel

World Energy Consumption by the Transportation Sector, 1971-1996

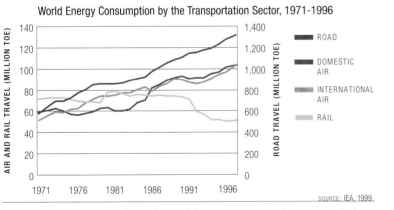

ROAD
DOMESTIC AIR
INTERNATIONAL AIR
RAIL

SOURCE: IEA, 1999.

Growing mobility has led to dramatic growth in energy use, greenhouse gas emissions, and other forms of pollution (see **Emissions**). In 1997, international marine shipping used 132 million tons of oil equivalent.[12] One indication of a world-on-the-move is the 80% increase in worldwide energy used for air travel and the nearly 120% rise in global energy for road transportation between 1971–1997. Road travel now represents 80% of total transportation energy use.[13] Most of the rising energy demand for road travel occurred in Eastern Europe, China, and Southeast Asia.[14]

Implications for Business

Increased mobility creates a 24-hour international business workday that puts workers on the road and accelerates economic and social change. Transportation also moves knowledge, disease, threats to public safety, and social unrest. Mobility opens market opportunities yet also allows entry of new competitors. Sustainable mobility is a major area of business investment and innovation as companies race to create affordable and efficient alternative fuel vehicles for freight and transit systems. In addition to designing efficient technologies, business plays a role along with the public sector in realizing easy and equal access to mobility. New technologies will only work in concert with changes in the way public institutions address the real costs of mobility-related infrastructure and energy use. Locating business activities near public transport, creating links between existing transport hubs, and providing incentives to employees to use public transit systems help encourage the use and development of energy-efficient public transport.

Access to telephones and the Internet is expanding quickly, although access is still limited in many parts of the world. As the Internet grows, it knits together markets and communities, facilitates the worldwide exchange of knowledge and services, and the movement of people and goods. The application of information and communication technologies helps the private sector launch new enterprises, reduce the costs of business transactions, and improve efficiency throughout the supply chain. Digital networks can improve productivity and enable people to participate in decisions that affect their lives — from natural resource use to politics. In the developing world, these technologies can enable billions of people to participate in the world economy by breaking down the spatial barriers between people and distant markets and employers (see **Labor**). Information and communication technologies promise significant opportunities for developing countries to create new development paths. Companies are creating new business models to connect rural villages with low-cost wireless technologies, to enable efficient micro-lending by using information technology, and to establish multi-purpose Internet centers for basic education, workforce training, small business lending, and agricultural information.[1] The Internet also enables the creation of new service businesses, from back office information processing to customer call centers; enterprises that can provide alternative livelihoods to traditional manufacturing and resource extraction industries.

Access to information and communication technologies enables economic opportunities.

Facts

- More than half the world's citizens have never used a telephone, 7% have access to a personal computer, and only 4% have access to the Internet.[2]

- Today, over 400 million people use the Internet, having grown from less than 20 million only 5 years ago. By 2005, there are forecast to be 1 billion Internet users.[3]

- In 2000 there were 214 countries connected to the Internet — up from 60 in 1993 and just 8 in 1988.[4]

- Internet use has been expanding in Latin America by more than 30% per year since 1998.[5]

- Estimates of global electronic commerce in 2000 range considerably, but most estimates are near US$200 billion.[6]

- The lion's share of e-commerce dollars is the business-to-business sector, which is expected to reach US$1.2 trillion to US$10 trillion by 2003.[7]

- In the United States, 20 hours of Internet access per month costs about 1% of the average income, compared to 15% in Mexico, 278% in Bangladesh, and 614% in Madagascar.[8]

Who Is Using The Web?

Total Number of Internet Users (in Millions), 2000

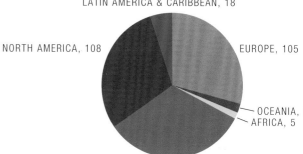

LATIN AMERICA & CARIBBEAN, 18
NORTH AMERICA, 108
EUROPE, 105
OCEANIA,
AFRICA, 5
ASIA, 118

SOURCE: International Telecommunications Union, 20

North America, Europe, and Asia each currently have about 100 milli Web users.[9] The approximate penetration rates (users per 1,000 peop of 35% in North America are significantly higher than those in Euro (14%), Asia (3%), Latin America (3%), and Africa (1%).[10] As this "digi divide" closes, proportionately more Internet use will be in developi countries, although Internet access may remain out of reach of most the world's poor for decades.

Emergence Of A Wired World

Number of PCs, Telephone Lines, and Mobile Phones per 1,000 People, 1988-1998

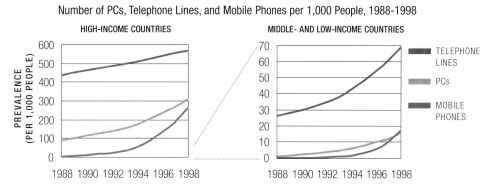

SOURCE: World Bank, 2000.

Though starting from a low base, connectivity via phones, and computers is growing fastest in the developing countries.[11] The application of information technologies and telecommunications promises to help emerging economies leapfrog traditional development patterns in favor of high-tech and high-efficiency economic pathways (see **Privatization**). However, Internet users need to be literate and it will be more difficult to surmount the problem of illiteracy in regions such as South Asia and Sub-Saharan Africa (see **Education**).

More than half the world's citizens have never used a telephone, 7% have access to a personal computer, and only 4% have access to the Internet.

Internet Hosts Are Booming Worldwide

Number of Internet Hosts per 10,000 People, 1994-2000

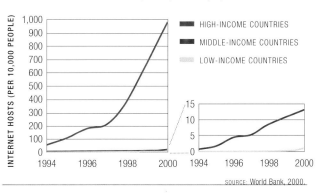

SOURCE: World Bank, 2000.

Worldwide, the number of Internet hosts per 10,000 people — a rough indicator of the "size" of the web — grew 500% from 1996 to 2000. High-income countries completely dominate this indicator, with nearly 1,000 hosts per 10,000 people; middle-income countries have about 13 hosts per 10,000 people, and low-income countries only 0.5.[12] There are regional exceptions such as Latin America and the Caribbean where there are now 30 hosts per 10,000 people. In developing regions, however, every connection may serve many members of a single community.

Implications for Business

The communications revolution can power the transition from a natural resource-based economy to a knowledge-based economy. Digital technologies can create gains in transactional efficiency, improved manufacturing controls, alternatives to paper, and energy-efficient logistics and production — helping businesses to become more environmentally sound and providing the means to inform purchasers about ecological impacts of products.[13] Connectivity can connect the world's poor to the international economy and to entrepreneurial and educational opportunities. Innovative use of the Internet, combined with software designed for illiterate users, and low-cost, solar-powered wireless devices, is already increasing incomes in developing countries.[14] Emerging communications technologies also help balance power between people, corporations, and nations by enabling businesses, government, and civil society to scrutinize each other and share information. However, the Internet may also create a negative "rebound effect." Lower costs and successful economic development will increase gross consumption levels and environmental impacts unless there is product and process innovation for sustainable production and consumption.[15] Also, if steps are not taken to ensure wide access to digital technologies, the Internet may exacerbate existing inequalities and strengthen monopolies.

The global labor force is growing and more women are moving from the informal to the formal labor sector as part of the transition of developing economies from an agricultural base to a manufacturing and service base.[1] Nearly all the projected growth in the labor force by 2025 will come from low- and middle-income countries and many of these new workers will need the skills demanded by manufacturing, technology, and information-based industries. Global competition enabled by more open trade, foreign direct investment and privatization, outsourcing of manufacturing, and growth of export-related activities spell a mixed future for laborers around the world — there will be employment losses in some areas and growth in others. Yet these changes also serve to raise the advantage that education provides to workers and create more opportunities for women.[2]

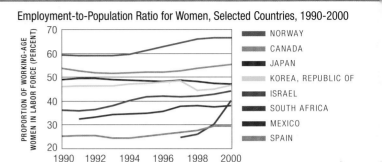

Closing The Gender Gap In Labor Markets

Employment-to-Population Ratio for Women, Selected Countries, 1990-2000

NORWAY
CANADA
JAPAN
KOREA, REPUBLIC OF
ISRAEL
SOUTH AFRICA
MEXICO
SPAIN

SOURCE: ILO, 200

Women's participation in the labor force is lowest in the Middle East and North Africa and is highest Sub-Saharan and Asian-Pacific economies, and in Norway and Sweden. In most countries the propo tion of the working-age male population that is employed ranges from 60-70%. However, men are muc more likely to be employed than women; the employment gender gap in developed countries average 18%, only 12% in transition economies, and 36% in the Middle East and North Africa. Of the 5 economies for which the International Labour Organization (ILO) has data for the 1990s, the emplo ment-to-population ratio declined for men and rose for women. In most countries, women have high unemployment than men due to employment pauses for childrearing, fewer occupational options, low levels of education and skills training, and layoffs due to less seniority (see **Education**).[3]

As economies become service-based, women are a growing part of the formal labor force

Facts

- In developed countries, the working age population (15-60 years) will shrink from approximately 740 million to 690 million people between 2000 and 2025. In the developing world, the working age population will increase 43% from approximately 3 billion to 4 billion people.[4]

- Approximately 50% of women are employed in the formal labor force and comprise one third of all workers. However, women earn about two thirds of what men earn in comparable jobs, and less than one fifth of total wages go to women.[5]

- In 1998, service sector jobs accounted for 64% of all jobs in the OECD countries.[6]

- The OECD estimated in 2000 that in the Information & Communication Technology sector there was a shortage of 850,000 technical staff in the United States and 2 million in Europe.[7]

New Doors Open For Women

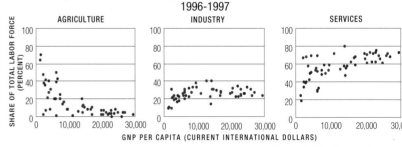

Percentage of Labor Force Employed in Various Sectors vs. Gross National Product, 1996-1997

AGRICULTURE   INDUSTRY   SERVICES

SHARE OF TOTAL LABOR FORCE (PERCENT)

GNP PER CAPITA (CURRENT INTERNATIONAL DOLLARS)

SOURCE: World Bank, World Development Indicators, 200

As economies develop, fewer people are employed in agriculture and more in positions tha require advanced skills and training in industry and services; the distribution of econom wealth in the world is strongly correlated with employment by sector. More women ar employed in agriculture in the Asian, Pacific, and Sub-Saharan nations, whereas develope and transition economies have more men involved in agricultural production. Worldwide, mor men are employed in the industrial sector while women generally find more employment in th service sector.[8] In the OECD countries, the ratio of women to men in the goods-producin sectors is 0.35:1, in the services sector the ratio is 1:1, and women outnumber men 1.8:1 social services such as health and education.[9]

Employing Young People Promotes Long-Term Growth And Stability

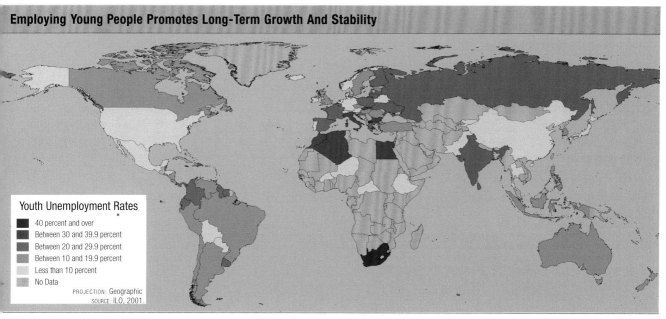

Youth Unemployment Rates
- 40 percent and over
- Between 30 and 39.9 percent
- Between 20 and 29.9 percent
- Between 10 and 19.9 percent
- Less than 10 percent
- No Data

PROJECTION: Geographic
SOURCE: ILO, 2001.

Youth (people ages 15-24) unemployment in most countries is about twice that of adult (ages 25-65) unemployment and is often substantially higher for young women than for young men. Youth employment is important for national and international development; unemployment at these early ages may harm future employment opportunity, damage social cohesion, and create unrest.[10]

In developed countries, the working age population will shrink from approximately 740 million to 690 million people between 2000 and 2025 but will increase in developing countries from about 3 billion to 4 billion people.

RELATED TRENDS	
Education	18
Wealth	12
Mobility	42

Imports Of Skilled Workers Grow

Non-Resident U.S. Visas Granted to Specialty Workers, 1985-1999

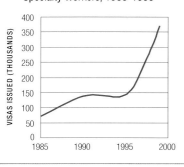

VISAS ISSUED (THOUSANDS)

H1B Visa Quotas, 1992-2000

YEAR	QUOTA	STATUS
1992	65,000	unfilled
1996	65,000	unfilled
1998	65,000	filled in September
1999	115,000	filled in June
2000	195,000	filled in March

SOURCE: US Department of Justice, 1998; OECD, 2001.

Demand for skilled labor is increasing, particularly in the high growth areas of business and professional services that are information technology-intensive. Though wages and unemployment data in the OECD countries do not currently reflect a shortage of skilled labor, most of the member countries have adapted policies to allow immigration of skilled foreign workers.[11] In recent years, the United States has allowed immigration of greater numbers of skilled workers and quickly filled the quotas.

Implications for Business

Increasing the skills of workers — particularly women — is crucial for business success in an integrated and competitive global economy. Labor capacity is not solely a matter of traditional education but is increasingly built through adult education and worker training within a context of career-long learning and career management.[12] Investing in workers boosts the living standards of households, increases productivity, and creates a broader customer base. Companies will successfully recruit and retain employees in competitive labor markets if they anticipate rising expectations of job quality, maternity benefits, flexible working hours, provision of child-care services, and access to professional training. Trade and the expansion of multinational companies creates an ethnically diverse labor force — an advantage to companies that want employees who can understand the needs of international and diverse markets and who can help companies locate operations where consumer and labor markets are growing.

Roles and Responsibilities

- ☑ **Democracy**
- ☐ **Accountability**
- ☐ **Privatization**

EARNING LICENSE-TO-OPERATE

Businesses must meet national rules and standards for commerce, and also international agreements, codes of conduct, and the standards of civil society at home and abroad. The public and many governments will hold businesses accountable to be socially responsible — that they will promote development that meets basic human needs, support democracy, share information, and be open to the scrutiny and input of civil society.

More people live in countries with elected democratic governments than at any other time in history. In many countries, the transition from state-controlled economies to market-based approaches has contributed to stable operating conditions and a common set of rules for international business competition (see **Privatization**). Countries are adopting international instruments of governance, including formal commitments to standards of human rights and environmental protection and gaining membership in the World Trade Organization (WTO). Democracies also benefit from an informed public, non-governmental organizations (NGOs) that are free to organize, and a media unfettered by restrictions of free speech — all conditions that help combat corruption (see **Accountability**). Today the challenge remains — to support democratic efforts to reduce corruption, promote sustainable development, and to increase the transparency of and participation in government processes.

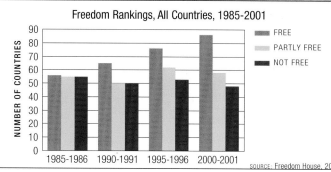

Political Rights And Civil Liberties Are Expanding

Freedom Rankings, All Countries, 1985-2001

SOURCE: Freedom House, 200

In 2001, the citizens of 86 countries worldwide could rely on a broad range o political rights and civil liberties; their countries were rated as "Free" in Freedor House's annual survey. The survey is based on political rights and civil libertie enjoyed by citizens, and not solely on political structure. Citizens in 58 "Part Free" countries live with more limited political rights and civil liberties. Limits o political and civil liberties can be caused by weak rule of law, single-party polit cal dominance, and inter-ethnic or religious violence. Basic political rights an civil liberties are denied people in 48 countries classified as "Not Free."[1]

Democracy spreads,
creating improved conditions
for market-based economies.

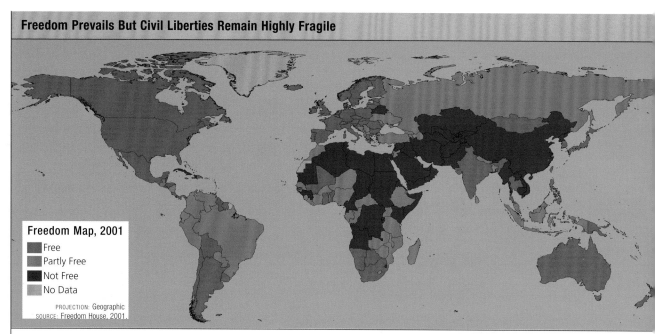

Freedom Prevails But Civil Liberties Remain Highly Fragile

Freedom Map, 2001
- Free
- Partly Free
- Not Free
- No Data

PROJECTION: Geographic
SOURCE: Freedom House, 2001.

The proportion of the world's population living in freedom has grown from 36% in 1981 to 41% in 2001. The proportion of the world's population lacking basic political rights and civil liberties has fallen from 43% to 36%. While gains in elected governments have been positive, in 66 coun- tries the improvements of civil liberties are lagging behind improvements of political rights.[2] Gains in freedom are especially threatened during financial and social crises, which often lead to non-democratic means to restore law and order.

Facts

- The number of democratic states in the world has grown from 22 democratic states out of 154 total countries (14.3%) in 1950, to 119 democratic states out of 192 total countries (62%) in 2000.[3]

- The number of countries that have ratified the six major human rights conventions and covenants has grown from 10% to half of all countries between 1990 and 2001.[4]

- The number of countries that have joined the General Agreement on Tariffs and Trade (GATT) and WTO has risen from 85 in 1980 to 134 in 1999.[5]

- Seventy-one percent (71%) of the world's exports now fall under WTO disciplines, with a growing share of exports coming from developing countries.[6]

Free Societies Enjoy Faster Growth

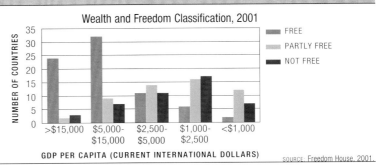

Wealth and Freedom Classification, 2001

SOURCE: Freedom House, 2001.

The median per capita GDP is almost seven times higher for the Freest countries than in the lowest category of Not Free countries. Almost all countries with per capita GDP higher than US$15,000 are Free, and most are Free where per capita GDP is between US$5,000 and US$15,000 (see **Wealth**). Countries that are freer grow — on average — more quickly as well. Notably, this is true even for the less affluent Free countries of less than US$5,000 per person per year (e.g. Benin, Bolivia, the Dominican Republic, El Salvador, India, and Papua New Guinea). Among countries with GDP per capita less than $5,000, the growth rates of Free, Partly Free, and Not Free countries in 1990–1998 were 3.23%, 1.47% and 1.41% respectively.[7] Countries with high economic growth rates and a Not Free classification, such as China, are uncommon.

> The number of democratic states in the world has grown from 22 democratic states out of 154 total countries in 1950, to 119 democratic states out of 192 total countries in 2000.

RELATED TRENDS	
Accountability	52
Education	18
Communications	44

Good Policies = Good Economies

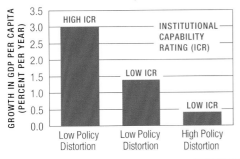

Association of GDP Growth Policy and Institutional Capability

SOURCE: World Bank, 1997.

Governments that have made changes in their macroeconomic policies and that have also made institutional reforms in the areas of social services, public works, banking, and overall regulations show much faster growth in GDP per capita.[8] Where the change toward electoral democracies is paralleled with progress toward freer civic institutions, an active and diverse media, a strengthened judiciary, and property rights, a solid foundation is created for long-term business operations.

Implications for Business

Democratic societies tend to offer the conditions for secure business operations, investment, and growth. In these societies, stakeholders and shareholders are holding corporations to a single high international standard. Business partnerships with dictatorial governments are scrutinized by an international network of NGOs, which makes the operations of ethical companies in non-democratic countries difficult and jeopardizes companies' license-to-operate at home and abroad. Companies will face the hard question of whether to operate in non-democratic environments and perhaps support democratic change through their own practices but risk harming their regional or international reputation. Ultimately, trends toward democracy, fair and transparent governance, and the development of global corporate standards are in the best interests of companies as they provide long-term benefits to reputation and operating freedom.

Civil society has a growing influence on government and business affairs. Many non-governmental organizations (NGOs) focus on making business and government activities more transparent to the public and more accountable to laws and to stakeholders who may be neither customers nor shareholders. Global business operations are scrutinized by NGOs that are well-organized, media savvy, active as shareholders, and connected by the Internet (see **Communications**). Businesses are responding to this public interest by reporting on environmental and social performance, and with innovative products and services that address public concerns about resource use, energy, and the environment. Others are engaging stakeholders in operational decisions and are partnering with NGOs to catalyze corporate change, to improve the bottom line, to protect reputation, and to earn license-to-operate in emerging markets.

The Rise Of Civil Society Organizations

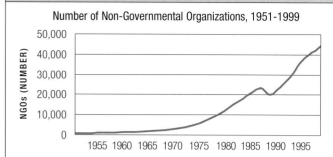

Number of Non-Governmental Organizations, 1951-1999

SOURCE: Union of International Associations, 199

The number of NGOs recorded by the Union of International Association has more than doubled since 1985 and is now over 40,000 organization working to improve the environment and the social welfare of people. Informal estimates put the number of NGOs at over one million.[2] Fuelin growth of these NGOs is more than US$150 billion in annual donations about 80% of that support is from individual donations and the balanc from bequests, foundations, and corporations.[3]

Civil society is demanding greater accountability and transparency from government and business.

Facts

■ About 10% of all development aid is channeled through NGOs, an amount that is expected to rise.[4]

■ Currently 2,091 NGOs hold consultative status at the United Nations, compared to 928 in 1991 and just 41 in 1948.[5]

■ Approximately 2,000 companies voluntarily report on their economic, environmental and social policies, practices, and performance — about 100 of these using a new international standard.[6]

■ The number of socially screened mutual funds in the United States increased from 168 funds in 1999 to 230 funds in 2001.[7]

■ The total of United States managed investment assets grew 22% from 1999 to 2001; socially screened assets under professional management grew by 36% in the same period.[8]

Shareholders Spotlight Corporate Responsibility

U.S. Shareholder Resolutions on Societal Issues, 1973-2000

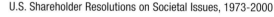

■ TOTAL RESOLUTIONS ■ PERCENTAGE OF RESOLUTIONS WITH SUPPORT ≥3% OF SHARES VOTED

SOURCE: IRRC, 2001b

Access to information through the Internet, expanded public participation in stock markets, and a broader definition of corporate social responsibility have led to increased shareholder activism, pressure for corporate disclosures, and new stock investment strategies.[9] Regulations that allow greater shareholder power and require disclosure are spreading in world equity markets. The Investor Responsibility Research Center has tracked shareholder resolutions in the United States since 1973 on social issues (e.g., diversity, human rights, environment, equal employment, and labor standards) and the number of resolutions that receive the 3% support needed to resubmit the resolution. The average level of support for these shareholder resolutions has risen steadily from 5% in the 1970s to today's level of about 9%.[10]

Combatting Corruption: A Win-Win for Business And Society

Transparency International's Corruption Perceptions Index, 2001

COUNTRY RANK		CORRUPTION INDEX	COUNTRY RANK		CORRUPTION INDEX
1.	Finland	9.9	91.	Bangladesh	0.4
2.	Denmark	9.5	90.	Nigeria	1.0
3.	New Zealand	9.4	88.	Uganda	1.9
4.	Iceland	9.2	88.	Indonesia	1.9
4.	Singapore	9.2	84.	Kenya, Bolivia Cameroon, Azerbaijan	2.0

SOURCE: Transparency International, 2001.

Business Registration Procedure: Association with Corruption and Income, 1999

[Bar chart: Index of Corruption (higher=more corrupt) and Average Per Capita GDP ($US thousands) by Business Registration Procedures (number): 1-5, 6-10, 11-15, >16]

CORRUPTION INDEX   AVERAGE PER CAPITA GDP

SOURCE: World Bank, 2001.

The Corruption Perceptions Index developed by Transparency International is an example of scrutiny by civil society. By surveying expatriate business executives, managers, and other experts, Transparency International ranks countries from 10 (highly clean) to 0 (highly corrupt). OECD countries generally rank high, with Russia a notable exception. Many developing countries such as Indonesia, Kenya, Nigeria, and Pakistan, all rank low with scores below 2.5.[11] Corruption is inconvenient and expensive. Excessive business regulations are associated with higher corruption and are more likely to be found in poorer countries (see **Democracy**). Such complex procedural systems also deter development of new businesses and competition and contribute to the abuse of power.[12]

Currently 2,091 NGOs hold consultative status at the United Nations, compared to 928 in 1991 and just 41 in 1948.

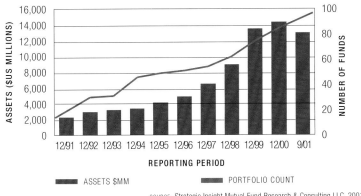

RELATED TRENDS	
Communications	44
Consumption	22
Wealth	12

Socially Responsible Investment Raises The Bar

Socially Screened Mutual Funds Excluding Variable Annuities, 1991-Sept 2001

[Chart: Assets ($US Millions) and Number of Funds by reporting period 12/91, 12/92, 12/93, 12/94, 12/95, 12/96, 12/97, 12/98, 12/99, 12/00, 9/01]

ASSETS $MM   PORTFOLIO COUNT

SOURCE: Strategic Insight Mutual Fund Research & Consulting LLC, 2001.

Investment based upon social criteria is rising in the United States, United Kingdom, Europe, and Japan. Part of the total invested assets are the public mutual funds that explicitly market themselves for social responsibility screens; the number of funds and their assets under management have grown five-fold in the last decade in the United States.[13] The number of socially screened funds doubled in the 1990s in the United Kingdom and total assets increased ten-fold.[14] The most common investment screens in the United States in 1999 were tobacco (96%), gambling (86%), weapons (81%), alcohol (83%), and the environment (79%).[15] The US$2.34 trillion in all portfolios in 2001 that include social criteria is 12% of total managed assets in the United States.[16]

Implications for Business

Rising public involvement in government and business affairs is seen in the growth and activism of non-governmental organizations, and in pressures to disclose environmental and social performance to investors. Civil society creates pressures for business to be more open and transparent in the way it deals with the public, government, other businesses, and local communities. International NGOs ensure that corporate activities anywhere in the world are under stakeholder and shareholder scrutiny. Failure to perform responsibly in a distant market or along the supply chain or in the launch of new products and technologies may erode corporate reputation and harm competitive position in core markets and in equity markets. Active engagement with stakeholders and documented good performance can protect license-to-operate, drive product and service innovation, reduce legal liabilities, and improve business strategy.

In the past decade, private sector investment in low- and middle-income countries has been growing quickly and governmental development aid has been on the wane. Governments are looking more and more to privatization as they seek to reform economies, reduce deficits, attract investments, liberalize and expand equity markets, and improve efficiency. When the private sector acquires state-owned enterprises, it often helps financial markets mature when that privatization includes public equity. Though governments still operate most infrastructure in low- and middle-income countries, the number of countries initiating privatization, the number of public projects with private sector participation, as well as the level of private sector investment are growing. Private sector investment may also transfer best practices for labor rights, resource efficiency, and environmental safety to transition and emerging economies.

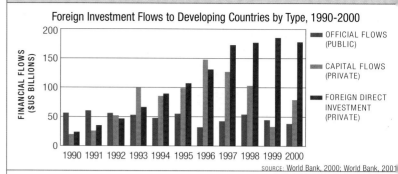

Private Investment In Developing Countries Dwarfs Governmental Aid

Foreign Investment Flows to Developing Countries by Type, 1990-2000

SOURCE: World Bank, 2000; World Bank, 2001

Government-to-government development assistance declined by nearly one third during the 1990s. Private capital flows (portfolio diversification to include foreign financial assets and private debt) expanded in the early 1990s and has since decreased. Foreign direct investment (investments to acquire a lasting management interest other than as an investor, e.g., equity capital and reinvestment of earnings), however, grew quickly through the entire decade. The Asian financial crisis of 1997 caused private flows to fluctuate and the current economic downturn may cause a relative decline, but long term private flows are still more than 80% of the total foreign financial flows.

Private sector investment is increasingly financing economic development.

Facts

- In 2000, official overseas development assistance (ODA) to developing countries totaled US$53.1 billion and foreign direct investment (FDI) was $120 billion; developing countries average about one fourth of international foreign development assistance.[1]

- In constant dollars, between 1970 and 1998, net inflows of foreign direct investment grew almost seven times faster than world GDP and four times faster than world exports of goods and services.[2]

- Foreign direct investment in developing countries has risen from about US$24 billion in 1990 to US$178 billion in 2000 as flows of official development aid declined from about US$55 billion to US$39 billion.[3]

- Between 1988 and 1995, revenues from the sale of state-owned-enterprises grew from US$2.6 billion to over US$21 billion. Latin America and East Asia generated the largest amount of revenues at 51% and 21% respectively.[4]

- In 1999, the primary sector (including petroleum, mining, agriculture, and forestry) accounted for US$18.1 billion (41% of the total) privatization revenues in emerging economies — almost entirely by oil and gas sales in Argentina, Brazil, India, Poland, and Russia.[5]

The Capital Bypasses The Poorest Nations

Private Capital Flows to Low- and Middle-Income Economies, 1990-2000

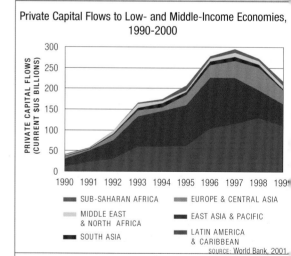

- SUB-SAHARAN AFRICA
- MIDDLE EAST & NORTH AFRICA
- SOUTH ASIA
- EUROPE & CENTRAL ASIA
- EAST ASIA & PACIFIC
- LATIN AMERICA & CARIBBEAN

SOURCE: World Bank, 2001.

Fifteen countries accounted for 83% of private capital flows to developing countries in 1997 and these are all middle-income countries — increased capital flows may have actually widened the income gap among countries. The Middle East and North Africa, Sub-Saharan Africa, and South Asia each received less than 5% of private capital flows and foreign direct investment in the 1990s.[6]

What Sectors Are Privatized?

Privatization by Major Sectors in Developing Countries. 1990-1999

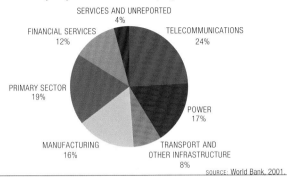

SERVICES AND UNREPORTED
4%
FINANCIAL SERVICES
12%
TELECOMMUNICATIONS
24%
PRIMARY SECTOR
19%
POWER
17%
MANUFACTURING
16%
TRANSPORT AND
OTHER INFRASTRUCTURE
8%

SOURCE: World Bank, 2001.

About US$316 billion of revenue has been generated by developing country privatization in the 1990s.[7] Investment of this magnitude and revenues to governments can have significant implications for people's well-being and the environment. The infrastructure and the primary sectors generated the greatest share of privatization revenues. Telecommunications has accounted for about one quarter of privatization revenue in non-OECD countries and one third of the revenues in OECD countries.[8]

Latin America And East Asia Attract Business

Investment in Private or Partial-Private Infrastructure Projects in Developing Countries, 1990 -1998 (1998 $US Billions)

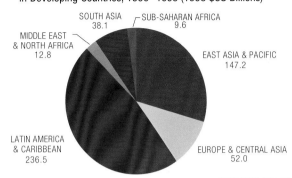

SOUTH ASIA
38.1
SUB-SAHARAN AFRICA
9.6
MIDDLE EAST
& NORTH AFRICA
12.8
EAST ASIA & PACIFIC
147.2
LATIN AMERICA
& CARIBBEAN
236.5
EUROPE & CENTRAL ASIA
52.0

SOURCE: World Bank, 1999.

Private activity — as measured by investment in infrastructure projects in which the private sector assumed operating risk during the project's development or operation — multiplied six-fold to over US$100 billion in the 1990s. The vast majority of private investment and projects occurred in Latin America and the Caribbean, or East Asia and the Pacific within two sectors: telecommunications and energy.[9]

Foreign direct investment in developing countries has risen from about US$24 billion in 1990 to US$178 billion in 2000 as official development aid declined from about US$55 billion to US$39 billion.

Privatization Bolsters Equity Markets

Global Amounts Raised from Privatization, 1990-2000

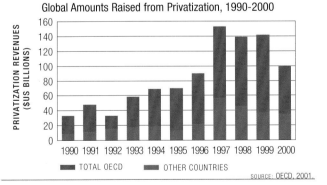

PRIVATIZATION REVENUES
($US BILLIONS)

TOTAL OECD   OTHER COUNTRIES

SOURCE: OECD, 2001.

Private investment activity can be seen in both the direct accounting of investment flows and by the revenues to governments from the sale of state-owned enterprises. OECD countries accounted for 70% of the past decade's privatization sales, two thirds of which are through public offerings. Though most of the approximately US$300 billion of asset privatizations in non-OECD countries in the last decade were not public sales, those that were marked milestones in their domestic equity market development.[10]

Implications for Business

Privatization has given business a greater say in the developing world's economic future.[11] The private sector has eclipsed but not replaced government as the major financier of development but still does not serve the poorest nations. Privatization focuses more attention upon the behavior of corporations and on the conditions that allow their license-to-operate. The expectation of the private ownership is to upgrade technologies, practices, and performance. Inconsistent standards among domestic and foreign subsidiaries are becoming increasingly difficult to justify and to maintain. Still, the state retains significant influence over the economic and social well-being of developing countries and private sector enterprises will have to adjust to an emerging partnership between the public and private sectors. Projections of population and economic growth mean that the investment opportunities of the past decade may be just a fraction of the potential future privatization markets.

Tomorrow's Market

POPULATION

1 U.N. Population Division (UNPD). 2000. *World Population Prospects: The 2000 Revision*. New York: UNPD.

2 This publication uses terms following the convention of the source of the data: e.g., developed and developing country as used by the United Nations' agencies and the World Bank's designations of low, medium, and high-income countries.

3 UNPD. 2000.

4 Ibid.

5 Ibid.

6 U.N. Population Division (UNPD). 1998. *Sex and Age Quinquennial 1950-2050, Description of the Dataset: The 1998 Revision*. New York: UNPD.

7 U.N. Population Division (UNPD). 1999. *World Population Prospects: The 1998 Revision*. New York: UNPD.

8 UNPD. 2000.

9 World Bank. 2001a. *World Development Indicators 2001*. Washington, DC: The World Bank.

10 UNPD. 2000.

11 U.N. Population Division (UNPD). 1999. Demographic Indicators, 1950-2050 (1998 revision on diskette) (UNPD, New York).

12 World Bank. 2001b. *World Development Indicators 2001*, on CD-ROM. Washington, DC: The World Bank.

13 UNPD. 1998.

■ **World Population by Income Group:** UNPD. 2000.

■ **Fertility Rates:** UNPD. 1998.

■ **World Population by Income Group:** World Bank. 2001b.

■ **Population Distribution by Age:** UNPD. 1998.

WEALTH

1 Hanmer, L., J. Healey, F. Naschold. 2000. "Will Growth Halve Global Poverty by 2015?" Overseas Development Institute (ODI) Poverty Briefing. Online at: http://www.odi.org/uk/briefing/pov8.html.

2 World Bank. 2001a. *World Development Indicators 2001*, on CD-ROM. Washington, DC: The World Bank.

3 Ibid.

4 World Bank. 2001b. *World Development Indicators 2001*. Washington, DC: The World Bank.

5 Milanovic, B. and S. Yitzhaki. 2001. *Decomposing World Income Distribution: Does the World have a Middle Class?* Washington, DC: The World Bank.

6 Milanovic, B. "True World Income Distribution, 1988 and 1993: First Calculation Based on Household Surveys Alone," World Bank Development Research Group Working Paper (The World Bank: Washington DC).

7 World Bank. 2001c. *World Development Report 2000/2001: Attacking Poverty*. Oxford University Press: World Bank.

8 World Bank. 2000. *World Development Indicators 2000*. Washington, DC: The World Bank.

■ **Gross Domestic Product Per Capita:** World Bank. 2001a.

■ **Map of 1998 Gross Domestic Product Per Capita:** World Resources Institute in collaboration with the U.N. Development Programme, the U.N. Environment Programme, and the World Bank. 2000. *World Resources 2000-2001: People and Ecosystems; the Fraying Web of Life*. Washington, DC: WRI. Available online at: http://www.wri.org/wr2000.

■ **Selected Poverty Rates:** World Bank. 2000.

■ **Distribution of Income:** World Bank. 2001a.

NUTRITION

1 Pinstrup-Andersen, P., R. Pandya-Lorch, and M. Rosegrant. 1999. "World Food Prospects: Critical Issues for the Early Twenty-First Century," 2020 Food Policy Report (International Food Policy Research Institute (IFPRI), Washington, DC).

2 Food and Agricultural Organization of the United Nations (FAO). 2000. *The State of Food Insecurity in the World*. Italy: FAO.

3 Food and Agricultural Organization of the United Nations (FAO). 2001. FAOSTAT On-line Statistical Service. Rome: FAO. Available online at: http://apps.fao.org.

4 Ibid.

5 FAO. 2000.

6 Pinstrup-Andersen, P. 1999.

7 Ross, J. and S. Horton. 1998. *Economic Consequences of Iron Deficiency*. Ottawa: Micronutrient Initiative.

8 U.N. Children's Fund (UNICEF). 2001. *The State of the World's Children 2001*. Available online at: http://www.unicef.org/sowc01; and U.N. Population Division (UNPD). 1998. *Sex and Age Quinquennial 1950-2050: The 1998 Revision*. New York: UNPD.

9 U.N. Children's Fund (UNICEF). 1998. *State of the World's Children 1998*. Available online at: http://www.unicef.org/sowc98/.

10 U.N. Administrative Committee on Coordination/Sub-Committee on Nutrition (ACC/SCN). 2000. *Fourth Report on the World Nutrition Situation*. Geneva: ACC/SCN in collaboration with IFPRI.

11 FAO. 2001; and U.N. Population Division (UNPD). 1999. Annual Populations 1950-2050 (1998 revision on diskette) (UNPD, New York).

12 World Bank. 2001. *World Development Indicators 2001*. Washington, DC: The World Bank.

■ **Undernourishment in Developing Countries:** FAO. 2000.

■ **Number and Percentage of Children Under Five:** UNICEF. 2001; and UNPD. 1998.

■ **Cereal Yields, World and Selected Regions:** FAO. 2001.

■ **Average Yields of Selected Cereals:** Ibid.

■ **Food Expenditures as a Percentage of Per Capita Income:** World Bank. 2001.

HEALTH

1 United Nations AIDS (UNAIDS) and World Health Organization (WHO). 2000. *AIDS Epidemic Update: December 2000*. Switzerland: UNAIDS and WHO.

2 U.N. Population Division (UNPD). 1998a. World Population Prospects (1998 revision on diskette) (UNPD, New York).

3 World Resources Institute in collaboration with the U.N. Development Programme, the U.N. Environment Programme, and the World Bank. 1998. *World Resources 1998-99: A Guide to the Global Environment*. New York: Oxford University Press.

4 World Health Organization (WHO). 2000. "Tuberculosis," Fact Sheet No. 104 (WHO, Geneva). Available online at: http://www.who.int/inf-fs/en/fact104.html.

5 United Nations AIDS (UNAIDS) and World Health Organization (WHO). 2001. *AIDS Epidemic Update: December 2001*. Switzerland: UNAIDS and WHO. Available online at: http://www.unaids.org/epidemic_update/report_dec01.

6 UNAIDS and WHO. 2001.

7 World Bank. 1999. *Curbing the Epidemic: Governments and the Economics of Tobacco Control*. Washington, DC: The World Bank. Available online at: http://www1.worldbank.org/tobacco/reports.htm.

8 UNPD. 1998a.

9 World Health Organization (WHO). 1999. *World Health Report 1999: Making a Difference*. Geneva: WHO. Available online at: http://www.who.int/whr/2001/archives/1999/en/index.htm.

10 UNAIDS and WHO. 2000.

11 World Health Organization (WHO). 2001. *HIV/AIDS in Asia and the Pacific Region*. Geneva: WHO.

12 UNAIDS and WHO. 2000.

■ **Life Expectancy by Region:** UNPD. 1998a.

■ **Life Expectancy, World and Selected Countries:** U.N. Population Division (UNPD). 1998b. World Population Prospects (1998 revision on diskette) (UNPD, New York).

■ **Cause of Death in Selected Regions:** World Health Organization (WHO). 2000. *World Health Report 2000*. Geneva: WHO. Available online at: http://www.who.int/whr/2001/archives/2000/en/index.htm.

■ **Leading Infectious Killers:** WHO. 1999.

EDUCATION

1 U.N. Educational, Scientific and Cultural Organization (UNESCO). 2000. *UNESCO Statistical Yearbook 1999*. Paris: UNESCO and White Plains: Bernan Press. Available online at: http://www.uis.unesco.org/en/stats/stats0.htm.

2 International Labour Organization (ILO). 2001. *Key Indicators of Labor Market 2001-2002*, on CD-ROM. International Labor Office, Geneva.

3 U.N. Educational, Scientific and Cultural Organization (UNESCO). 2000. *Education for All 2000 Assessment: Year 2000 Assessment*. Nimes, France: UNESCO. Available online at: http://www.unesco.org/education/efa/efa_2000_assess/index.shtr

4 Ibid.

5 World Bank. 2001. *World Development Report 2000/2001: Attack Poverty*. Oxford University Press: World Bank.

6 World Resources Institute in collaboration with the U.N. Developme Programme, the U.N. Environment Programme, and the World Ban 1998. *World Resources 1998-99: A Guide to the Global Environment*. New York: Oxford University Press.

7 International Consultative Forum on Education for All. 2000. *Education for All: Status and Trends 2000*. Paris: UNESCO.

8 UNESCO. 2000.

9 Gross enrollment ratios can exceed 100% due to the inclusion of over-aged and under-aged students. See U.N. Educational, Scientif and Cultural Organization (UNESCO). 1998. *UNESCO Statistical Yearbook*. Paris: UNESCO and White Plains: Bernan Press.

10 International Labour Organization (ILO). 2001. *Key Indicators of Labour Market 2001-2002*, on CD-ROM. Geneva: ILO; and Organization for Economic Development (OECD). 2001. *Education a Glance: OECD Indicators*. Paris: OECD.

11 World Bank. 2001a. *World Development Indicators 2001*. Washington, DC: The World Bank.

12 Colclough, C. and K.M. Lewin. 1993. *Educating All the Children*. (Oxford University Press) cited from Population Council (2001) "Accelerating Girls' Education: A Priority for Governments," Online a http://www.popcouncil.org/gfd/girlseducation.html.

■ **Adult Literacy Rates:** U.N. Educational, Scientific and Cultural Organization (UNESCO). 2000. *UNESCO Statistical Yearbook 1999*. Paris: UNESCO and White Plains: Bernan Press. Available online at: http://www.uis.unesco.org/en/stats/stats0.htm.

■ **Secondary School Gross Enrollment:** U.N. Educational, Scientific and Cultural Organization (UNESCO). 1998. *UNESCO Statistical Yearbook 1998*. Paris: UNESCO and White Plains: Bernan Press.

■ **Average Earnings:** Organization for Economic Development (OECD) 2001. *Education at a Glance: OECD Indicators*. Paris: OECD.

■ **Fertility Rates:** The World Bank. 2001b. *World Development Indicators 2001*, on CD-ROM. Washington, DC: The World Bank; ar U.N. Educational, Scientific and Cultural Organization (UNESCO). 1998. *UNESCO Statistical Yearbook*. Paris: UNESCO and White Plains: Bernan Press.

Innovation

CONSUMPTION

1 World Bank. 2001. *World Development Indicators 2001*, on CD-ROM. Washington, DC: The World Bank.

2 Ibid.

3 Delgado, C., M. Rosegrant, et al. 1999. "Livestock to 2020: The Ne Food Revolution," Food, Agriculture, and the Environment Discussio Paper No. 28. (International Food Policy Research Institute (IFPRI), Washington, DC).

4 World Bank. 2001.

5 World Bank. 2001; and U.N. Population Division (UNPD). 1999. Annual Populations, 1950-2050 (1998 revision on diskette) (UNPD, New York).

6 WRI calculation based on Food and Agricultural Organization of the United Nations (FAO). 2001. FAOSTAT On-line Statistical Service. Rome: FAO. Available online at: http://apps.fao.org.

7 Food and Agricultural Organization of the United Nations (FAO). 2001. FAOSTAT On-line Statistical Service. Rome: FAO. Available online at: http://apps.fao.org.

■ **Household Consumption:** World Bank. 2000. *World Development Indicators 2000*. Washington, DC: The World Bank.

■ **Televisions per 1,000 People:** World Bank. 2001.

■ **Passenger Cars:** Ibid.

■ **Meat Consumption:** FAO. 2001.

ENERGY

1 Intergovernmental Panel on Climate Change (IPCC). 2001. *Climate Change 2001: The Scientific Basis*. Cambridge: Cambridge University Press.

2 U.N. Development Programme (UNDP). 2001. *Human Development Report 2001*. New York and Oxford: Oxford University Press. Available online at: http://www.undp.org/hdr2001.

3 Logan, J., A. Frank, J. Feng, and I. John. 1999. "Climate Action in the United States and China," May 1999. Online at: http://www.pnl.gov/aisu/pubs/climactione.pdf.

4 Case A assumes high growth of income and technology, while Case B assumes more moderate growth. Case C predicts increased international cooperation with a focus on equity and energy efficiency, with higher economic and technological growth than Case B. See Nakićenović, N., A. Grübler, and A. McDonald, eds. 1998. *Global Energy Perspectives*. Cambridge: Cambridge University Press. Available online at: http://www.iiasa.ac.at/cgi-bin/ecs/book_dyn/bookcnt.py.

5 Denman, J. 1998. *IEA Biomass Energy Data: System, Methodology and Initial Results*. Proceedings of the Conference on Biomass Energy: Data, Analysis and Trends, March 23-24. Paris. Energy Statistics Division, International Energy Agency (IEA). Available online at: http://www.iea.org/pubs/proc/files/bioend/index.htm; and U.N. Development Programme (UNDP). 2001. "World Energy Assessment: Energy and the Challenge of Sustainability," Online at: http://www.undp.org/seed/eap/activities/wea/drafts-frame.html.

6 NASA Goddard Institute for Space Studies Datasets and Images. 2000. "Global Surface Air Temperature Anomaly," Online at: http://www.giss.nasa.gov/data/update/gistemp/graphs/FigA.txt.

7 Woodard, C. 2001. "Wind Turbines Sprout from Europe to US," *Christian Science Monitor* 93(75):7.

8 PV Energy Systems, Inc. 2001. *PV World Market, 1975-2010*. Warrenton, VA: PV Energy Systems. Available online at: http://www.pvenergy.com.

9 IPCC. 2001.

10 International Energy Agency (IEA). 1999a. Energy Balances of Non-OECD Countries, 1960-1997 (on diskette) (OECD, Paris).

11 International Energy Agency (IEA). 1999b. Energy Balances of OECD Countries, 1960-1997 (on diskette) (OECD, Paris).

12 IEA. 1999b; and McVeigh, J., D. Burtraw, J. Darmstadter, and K. Palmer. 1999. "Winner, Loser or Innocent Victim: Has Renewable Energy Performed as Expected?" Research Report No. 7. Washington, DC: Renewable Energy Policy. Available online at http://www.repp.org.

13 World Resources Institute (WRI)/World Business Council for Sustainable Development (WBCSD). 2001. *The Greenhouse Gas Protocol*. Switzerland: WRI and WBCSD.

14 Margolick, M., and D. Russel. 2001. *Corporate Greenhouse Gas Reduction Targets*. Arlington, VA: Pew Center on Global Climate Change.

■ World Annual Energy Production: International Energy Agency (IEA). 2000. *World Energy Outlook 2000*. Paris: Organisation for Economic Co-Operation and Development (OECD) and the IEA.

■ Three Scenarios of Global Energy Consumption: Nakićenović, N. 1998.

■ Atmospheric Carbon Dioxide: Carbon Dioxide Information Analysis Center (CDIAC). 2001. "Current Greenhouse Gas Concentrations," Online at: http://cdiac.esd.ornl.gov.

■ Global Surface Air Temperature: NASA Goddard Institute for Space Studies Datasets and Images. 2000.

■ Global Solar and Wind Energy Production: International Energy Agency (IEA). 2000. *World Energy Outlook 2000*. Paris: Organisation for Economic Co-Operation and Development (OECD) and the IEA.

EMISSIONS

1 Organisation for Economic Co-Operation and Development (OECD). 1999. *OECD Environmental Data Compendium 1999*. Washington, DC: OECD.

2 Matthews, E. Amann, C., Bringezu, S., et al. 2000. *The Weight of Nations: Material Outflows from Industrial Economies*. Washington, DC: WRI.

3 U.N. Environment Programme (UNEP). 1999. *Global Environment Outlook 2000*. London: UNEP.

4 Vogan, C.R. 1996. "Survey of Current Business," U.S. Department of Commerce, Bureau of Economic Analysis. Online at: http://www.bea.gov/bea/an/0996eed/maintext.htm.

5 Organisation for Economic Co-Operation and Development (OECD). 2001. OECD *Environmental Outlook*. Paris: OECD.

6 Ibid.

7 U.N. Environment Programme (UNEP). 2000. *Natural Selection: Evolving Choices for Renewable Energy Technology and Policy*. Paris: UNEP; World Bank. 2001. *World Development Indicators 2001*. Washington, DC: The World Bank; and Healthy Cities Air Management Information System (Amis 2.0) 1998. World Health Organization (WHO): Geneva.

8 Programme for Monitoring and Evaluation of the Long-Range Transmission of Air Pollutants in Europe (EMEP). "Tables of anthropogenic emissions in the ECE region," Online at: http://www.emep.int/emis_tables/tab1.html.

9 McDonald, A. 1999. "Priorities for Asia: Combating Acid Deposition and Climate Change." *Environment* 41(3):4--20.

10 U.S. Environmental Protection Agency (EPA). 2001. "Toxic Release Inventory 1999," Online at: http://www.epa.gov/tri.

11 OECD. 2001.

12 United Nations Environment Programme (UNEP). 1999. *Production and Consumption of Ozone Depleting Substances: 1986-1998*. Nairobi: UNEP.

13 U.N. Environmental Programme (UNEP). 2001. "Persistent Organic Pollutants," Online at: http://www.chem.unep.ch/pops/default.html.

■ Emissions Sources for Selected Air Pollutants: OECD. 2001.

■ Concentration of Key Pollutants in Major Cities: World Bank. 2001; and Healthy Cities Air Management Information System (Amis 2.0) 1998.

■ SOx Emissions in Selected Countries: Programme for Monitoring and Evaluation of the Long-Range Transmission of Air Pollutants in Europe (EMEP). 2001. "EMEP Searchable Database," Online at: http://www.emep.int/emis_tables/tab1.html; and McDonald, A. 1999.

■ Toxic Releases in the United States: U.S. Environmental Protection Agency (EPA). 2001. "TRI Explorer: Chemical Report," Online at: http://www.epa.gov/triexplorer/chemical.htm.

■ Production of CFCs in Selected Countries: UNEP. 1999.

EFFICIENCY

1 Steel Recycling Institute (SRI). "Buy Recycled with Recyclable Steel," Online at: http://www.recycle-steel.org/index2.html.

2 European Aluminum Association (EAA). 2001. "Aluminum Industry in Europe: Key Statistics for 2000," Online at: http://www.eaa.net/downloads/keystat00.pdf.

3 Food and Agricultural Organization of the United Nations (FAO). 2001. FAOSTAT On-line Statistical Service. Rome: FAO. Available online at: http://apps.fao.org.

4 Compromisso Empresarial Para Reciclagem (CEMPRE). Online at: http://www.cempre.org.br/ingles/frames/fr_fichastecnicas.html.

5 Adriaanse, A., S. Bringezu, A. Hammond, et al. 1997. *Resource Flows: The Material Basis of Industrial Economies*. Washington, DC: WRI; and Matthews, E. Amann, C., Bringezu, S., et al. 2000. *The Weight of Nations: Material Outflows from Industrial Economies*. Washington, DC: WRI.

6 Moll, S. 2001. "Material Flow Accounting: A Tool to Measure Progress in Resource Productivity," Annual Consultative Meeting with Industry Associations, Wuppertal Institute. Online at: http://www.uneptie.org/Outreach/business/2001-presentations.htm.

7 Matthews, E. Amann, C., Bringezu, S., et al. 2000. *The Weight of Nations: Material Outflows from Industrial Economies*. Washington, DC: WRI.

8 Organisation for Economic Co-Operation and Development (OECD). 2001. *OECD Environmental Outlook*. Paris: OECD.

9 Matthews, E. 2000.

10 FAO. 2001.

11 International Association for Energy-Efficient Lighting. 2000. *International Association for Energy-Efficient Lighting Newsletter, 2000*. Berkeley: International Association for Energy-Efficient Lighting.

■ Trends in Total Material Requirements: Moll, S. 2001.

■ Industrial Energy Use: WRI calculation based on World Bank. 2001. *World Development Indicators*, on CD-ROM. Washington, DC: The World Bank; International Energy Agency (IEA). 1999. Energy Balances of Non-OECD Countries, 1960-1997 (on diskette) (OECD, Paris); and International Energy Agency (IEA). 1999. Energy Balances of OECD Countries, 1960-1997 (on diskette) (OECD, Paris).

■ Examples of Efficiency Gains: OECD. 2001.

■ Total Paper Production: FAO. 2001.

Natural Capital

ECOSYSTEMS

1 World Bank. 2001. *World Development Indicators*, on CD-ROM. Washington, DC: The World Bank.

2 Bryant, D., L. Burke, J. McManus and M. Spalding. 1998. *Reefs at Risk: A Map-Based Indicator of Threats to the World's Coral Reefs*. Washington, DC: WRI.

3 Burke, L., Y. Kura, K. Kassem, et al. 2001. *Pilot Analysis of Global Ecosystems (PAGE): Coastal Ecosystems*. Washington, DC: WRI. Available online at http://www.wri.org/wr2000/coast_page.html; and Levitus, S., J. Antonov, J. Wang, et al. 2001. "Anthropogenic Warming of Earth's Climate System," *Science* 292(5515):267--271.

4 Wilkinson, C., O. Lindén, H. Cesar, et al. 1999. "Ecological and Socioeconomic Impacts of 1998 Coral Mortality in the Indian Ocean: An ENSO Impact and a Warning of Future Change?" *Royal Swedish Academy of Sciences* 28(2):188--196. Available online at: http://www.ambio.kva.se.

5 World Conservation Monitoring Centre (WCMC). 1999. WCMC Species Database (unpublished data) (Cambridge, UK: WCMC) as reported in World Resources Institute in collaboration with the U.N. Development Programme, the U.N. Environment Programme, and the World Bank. 2000. *World Resources 2000-2001: People and Ecosystems: The Fraying Web of Life*. Washington, DC: WRI. Available online at: http://www.wri.org/wr2000.

6 World Conservation Union (IUCN). 2000. "2000 IUCN Red List on Threatened Species," Online at: http://www.redlist.org/info/tables/table1b.html.

7 WRI. 2000.

8 Revenga, C., J. Brunner, et al. 2000. *Pilot Analysis of Global Ecosystems (PAGE): Freshwater Systems*. Washington, DC: WRI. Available online at: http://www.wri.org/wr2000/freshwater_page.html.

9 WRI. 2000.

10 ten Kate, K. and S. Laird. 1999. *The Commercial Use of Biodiversity: Access to Genetic Resources and Benefit-Sharing*. UK: Earthscan.

11 Palumbi, S.R. 2001. "Humans as the World's Greatest Evolutionary Force," *Science* 293(5536):1786-1791.

12 In many industrialized countries, forest area is increasing because of the natural conversion of former agricultural lands to forest as well as an increase in the area of tree plantations. Forest area is simultaneously being lost in these countries because of urbanization, new roads, and recreational facilities.

13 Food and Agriculture Organization of the United Nations (FAO). 2001. "State of the World's Forests 2001," Online at: http://www.fao.org/forestry/fo/fra/index_tables.jsp.

14 FAO. 2001.

15 Matthews, E., R. Payne, M. Rohweder, and S. Murray. 2000. *Pilot Analysis of Global Ecosystems (PAGE): Forest Ecosystems*. Washington, DC: WRI. Available online at: http://www.wri.org/wr2000/forests_page.html; and R.T. Watson et al. Intergovernmental Panel on Climate Change (IPCC). "Land Use, Land-Use Change And Forestry," Online at: http://www.grida.no/climate/ipcc/land_use/003.htm.

16 Food and Agriculture Organization of the United Nations (FAO). 1999. "FAO Fishery Statistics Database: FISHSTAT Plus Software," Online at: http://www.fao.org/DOCREP/003/X8002E/x8002e04.htm.

17 Food and Agriculture Organization of the United Nations (FAO). 1999. "FAO Fishery Statistics Database: FISHSTAT Plus Software," Online at: http://www.fao.org/fi/statist/fisoft/fishplus.asp#Features.

18 Food and Agriculture Organization of the United Nations (FAO). 2000. "Forest Resource Assessment," Online at: http://www.fao.org/forestry/fo/fra/index_tables.jsp.

■ Regional Coral Reef Area: Bryant, D. 1998.

■ Percentage Change in Forest Area: FAO. 2000.

■ Map of Period of Peak Catch: Food and Agriculture Organization of the United Nations (FAO). 1999. "FAO Fishery Statistics Database: FISHSTAT Plus Software;" and Food and Agriculture Organization of the United Nations (FAO). 1999. *Yearbook of Fishery Statistics— Capture Production 1997*. Vol. 84 FAO Fisheries Series No. 52. Rome, Italy: FAO as reported in Burke, L. 2001.

■ Certified Forest Area: FAO. 2000.

AGRICULTURE

1 Wood, S., K. Sebastian, S. Scherr. 2000. *Pilot Analysis of Global Ecosystems (PAGE): Agroecosystems Technical Report.* Washington, DC: WRI and IFPRI. Available online at: http://www.wri.org/wr2000/agroecosystems_page.html; and White, R., S. Murray, and M. Rohweder. 2000. *Pilot Analysis of Global Ecosystems (PAGE): Grassland Ecosystems.* Washington, DC: WRI. Available online at: http://www.wri.org/wr2000/grasslands_page.html.

2 Wood, S. 2000.

3 Ibid.

4 International Commission on Large Dams (ICOLD). 1998. *World Register of Dams 1998.* Paris, France: ICOLD; and World Commission on Dams (WCD). 2000. *Dams and Development: A New Framework for Decision-Making.* London, UK: Earthscan Publications Ltd.

5 Food and Agricultural Organization of the United Nations (FAO). 2001. FAOSTAT On-line Statistical Service. Rome: FAO. Available online at: http://apps.fao.org; and U.S. Department of Agriculture Production (USDA). 1999. *Production, Supply, and Distribution View.* Washington, DC: USDA. Available online at: http://usda.mannlib.cornell.edu/data-sets/international/93002/ and at http://earthtrends.wri.org.

6 World Bank. 2001. *World Development Indicators,* on CD-ROM. Washington, DC: The World Bank.

7 Wood, S. 2000.

8 Willer, H. and M. Yussefi. 2001. *Organic Agriculture Worldwide: Statistics and Future Prospects.* Germany: Stiftung Ökologie & Landbau. Available online at: http://www.soel.de/inhalte/publikationen/s_74_03_1.pdf; and Lohr, L. 2000. *Factors Affecting International Demand and Trade in Organic Food Products, Economic Research Service.* Washington, DC: US Department of Agriculture.

9 International Trade Centre UNCTAD/WTO. 1999. "Summary of Market Opportunities for Developing Countries," Online at: http://www.intracen.org/mds/sectors/organic/summary2.htm.

10 Food and Agriculture Organization of the United Nations (FAO). 1999. "FAO Fishery Statistics Database: FISHSTAT Plus Software," Online at: http://www.fao.org/fi/statist/fisoft/fishplus.asp#Features; and FAO. 2001.

■ Map of Severity of Soil Degradation: Oldeman, L.R., R.T.A. Hakkeling, and W.G. Sombroek. 1991. *World Map of the Status of Human Induced Soil Degradation: An Explanatory Note, Second revised edition.* Wageningen and Nairobi: International Soil Reference and Information Centre (ISRIC) and U.N. Environmental Programme (UNEP) as referenced in Wood, S. 2000.

■ Concentration of Nitrogenous Fertilizer Consumption: FAO. 2001.

■ Organic Retail Sales: Willer, H. 2001.

■ Aquaculture Production: FAO.1999.

FRESHWATER

1 Revenga, C., J. Brunner, et al. 2000. *Pilot Analysis of Global Ecosystems (PAGE): Freshwater Systems.* Washington, DC: WRI. Available online at: http://www.wri.org/wr2000/freshwater_page.html.

2 Revenga, C. 2000; and Stiassny, M.L. 1999. "The Medium is the Message: Freshwater Biodiversity in Peril," pp. 53-71 in *The Living Planet in Crisis: Biodiversity Science and Policy* (New York: Columbia University Press).

3 Harrison I.J. and M.L. Stiassny. 1999. "The quiet crisis: a preliminary listing of the freshwater fishes of the world that are extinct or 'missing in action'" p. 298 in *Extinctions in Near Time: Causes, Contexts, and Consequences* (Kluwer Academic/Plenum Publishers, New York).

4 Stanners, D. and P. Bordeau eds. 1995. *Europe's Environment: The Dobris Assessment.* Copenhagen, Denmark: European Environment Agency.

5 Foster, S., A. Lawrence, B. Morris. 1998. "Groundwater in Urban Development," World Bank Technical Paper No. 390 (The World Bank, Washington, DC).

6 Organisation for Economic Co-Operation and Development (OECD). 1999. *The Price of Water: Trends in OECD Countries.* Paris: OECD.

7 Withdrawals refer to the total volume of water removed from nonrenewable groundwater sources, river flows from other countries, and desalination plants, not counting evaporative losses from storage basins. Withdrawals may be returned to their source after use (e.g. for cooling). See World Meteorological Organization. 1997. "Comprehensive Assessment of the Freshwater Resources of the World," Online at: http://www.wmo.ch/web/homs/cfwadesc.html.

8 Postel, S. 1993. "Water and Agriculture," p. 56 in *Water Crisis: A Guide to the Worlds Fresh Water Resources* (Oxford University Press, New York).

9 Shiklomanov, I.A. 1997. *Comprehensive Assessment of the Freshwater Resources of the World: Assessment of Water Resources and Water Availability in the World.* Stockholm, Sweden: World Meteorological Organization and Stockholm Environment Institute.

10 Falkenmark, M. and C. Widstrand. 1992. *Population and Water Resources: A Delicate Balance.* Population Bulletin Vol. 47, No. 3. Washington, DC: Population Reference Bureau, Inc.

11 Revenga, C. 2000.

12 Postel, S. and A. Wolf. 2001. "Dehydrating Conflict." *Foreign Policy.* September/October 2001. Available online at: http://www.foreignpolicy.com/issue_SeptOct_2001/postel.html.

13 "Improved" water sources include household connections, public standpipes, boreholes, protected wells, and rainwater collection systems located less than 1 km from a person's home. See World Bank. 2001. *World Development Indicators 2001.* Washington, DC: The World Bank.

14 Van der Hoek, W., F. Konradsen, and W.A. Jehangir. 1999. "Domestic use of irrigation water: health hazard or opportunity?" *International Journal of Water Resources Development* 15(1/2):107-119.

15 Cosgrove, W.J. and F. Rijsberman. 2000. *World Water Vision 2000.* United Kingdom: Earthscan Publications Ltd.

■ Water Withdrawals by Sector: Shiklomanov, I.A. 1997.

■ Irrigated Cropland: Food and Agricultural Organization of the United Nations (FAO). 2001. FAOSTAT On-line Statistical Service. Rome: FAO. Available online at: http://apps.fao.org.

■ Map of Projected Renewable Water Supply: Center for International Earth Science Information Network (CIESIN). 2000. Columbia University; International Food Policy and Research Institute; World Resources Institute (WRI). Gridded Population of the World, Version 2. Palisades, NY: CIESIN, Columbia University. Available online at: http://sedac.ciesin.columbia.edu/plue/gpw/index.html; and Fekete, B., C.J. Vörösmarty, and W. Grabs. 1999. *Global, Composite Runoff Fields Based on Observed River Discharge and Simulated Water Balance.* Koblenz, Germany: WMO-GRDC as referenced in Revenga, C. 2000.

■ Access to an Improved Water Source: World Bank. 2001.

Connections

URBANIZATION

1 U.N. Population Fund (UNFPA). 1999. *The State of World Population 1999.* London: UNFPA. Available online at: http://www.unfpa.org/SWP/1999/thestate.htm.

2 U.N. Population Division (UNPD). 1999. World Population Prospects (1999 revision on diskette) (UNPD, New York).

3 Ibid.

4 UNPD. 1999; and World Bank. 2001. *World Development Indicators 2001.* Washington, DC: The World Bank.

5 UNPD. 1999.

6 Schwela, D. 1996. "Exposure to environmental chemicals relevant for respiratory hypersensitivity: global aspects." Toxicology Letters 86, 131-142.

7 U.N. Environment Programme (UNEP). 1999. *Global Environment Outlook 2000.* London: UNEP.

8 International Bank for Reconstruction and Development (IBRD)/The World Bank. 1999. *What a Waste: Solid Waste Management in Asia.* Washington, DC: IBRD. Available online at: http://www.worldbank.org/heml/fpd/urban/publicat/waste.pdf.

9 UNPD. 1999.

10 Hinrichsen, D. 1998. *Coastal Waters of the World: Trends, Threats, and Strategies.* Washington, DC: Island Press.

■ Percent of Total Population that is Urban: UNPD. 1999.

■ World Urban Population by City Size: Ibid.

■ The World's Largest Cities: Present, and Future: Ibid.

■ Map of the World's Largest Cities: Ibid.

■ Comparison of Urban-Rural Statistics: International Institute for Population Sciences (IIPS) and ORC Macro. 2000. *National Family Health Survey (NFHS-2), 1998-1999: India.* Mumbai, India: IIPS.

Available online at: http://www.nfhsindia.org/india.html; Bureau of Statistics [Tanzania] and Macro International Inc. 1997. *Tanzania Demographic and Health Survey 1996.* Calverton, MD: Bureau of Statistics and Macro International; National Committee for Population and Family Planning and The Population and Family Health Project. 1999. *Vietnam Demographic and Health Survey 1997.* Hanoi: National Committee for Population and Family Planning and The Population and Family Health Project; and World Bank. 2001.

MOBILITY

1 International Energy Agency (IEA). 2000a. *World Energy Outlook 2000.* Paris: OECD and IEA. Available online at: http://www.iea.org/weo/oilprod.jpg.

2 World Business Council on Sustainable Development (WBCSD). 2001. *Mobility 2001.* Boston: WBCSD. Available online at: http://www.wbcsdmobility.org/publications/mobility2001/pdf/english_full_report.pdf.

3 International Energy Agency (IEA). 1999. Energy Balances of OECD Countries, 1960-1997 (1999 revision of diskette) (OECD, Paris); an International Energy Agency (IEA). 2000. *World Energy Outlook 2000.* Paris: OECD and the IEA.

4 WBCSD. 2001.

5 UNAIDS. 2001. *Population Mobility and AIDS. UNAIDS Technical Update.* Geneva: UNAIDS. Available online at: http://www.unaids.org/publications/documents/specific/rufugees/JC513-PopulationTU-E.pdf.

6 WBCSD. 2001.

7 Ibid.

8 Organisation for Economic Co-Operation and Development (OECD). 2001. *OECD Environmental Outlook.* Paris: OECD.

9 World Bank. 2001. "Roads and Highways: Overview," Online at: http://www.worldbank.org/html/fpd/transport/roads_ss.htm.

10 World Bank. 2001a. *World Development Indicators 2001,* on CD-ROM. Washington, DC: The World Bank; and World Bank. 2000. *World Development Indicators 2000.* Washington, DC: The World Bank.

11 World Bank. 2001b. *World Development Indicators 2001.* Washington, DC: The World Bank.

12 International Energy Agency (IEA). 2000b. *Energy Balances of Non-OECD Countries, 1971-1997 Database.* Paris: OECD.

13 IEA. 2000b; and International Energy Agency (IEA). 1999. Energy Balances of OECD Countries, 1960-1997 (on diskette) (OECD, Paris)

14 IEA. 1999.

■ Ocean Shipping Demand: WBCSD. 2001.

■ Total Road Traffic: World Bank. 2001b.

■ Increase In Road Traffic: Ibid.

■ Global Number of Air Passengers: World Bank. 2000. *World Development Indicators,* on CD-ROM. Washington, DC: The World Bank.

■ World Energy Consumption: IEA. 2000b.

COMMUNICATIONS

1 Hammond, A.L. 2001. "Digitally Empowered Development." *Foreign Affairs* 80(2):96--107.

2 United Nations. 2001. *'We the Peoples:' The Role of the UN in the 21st Century.* United Nations Department of Public Information. Available online at: http://www.un.org/millennium/sg/report/full.htm; and World Bank. 2001a. *World Development Indicators 2001.* Washington, DC: The World Bank.

3 U.N. Development Programme (UNDP). 2001. *Human Development Report 2001.* New York and Oxford: Oxford University Press. Available online at: http://www.undp.org/hdr2001.

4 Ibid.

5 International Telecommunication Union (ITU). 2001. "Numbering Cyberspace: Recent Trends in the Internet World," Online at: http://www.itu.int./ITU-D/ict/update/pdf/update_1_01.pdf.

6 U.N. Conference on Trade and Development (UNCTAD). 2001. "E-Commerce and Development Report, 2001," Online at: http://www.unctad.org/en/pub/ps1ecdr01.en.htm.

7 UNDP. 2001.

8 SustainAbility. 2001. "Using the Internet to Implement the Triple Bottom Line," Online at: http://www.sustainability.com.

9 International Telecommunication Union (ITU). 2001. "Internet Indicators: Hosts, Users and Number of PCs," Online at: http://www.itu.int/ITU-D/ict/statistics/at_glance/Internet00.pdf.

10 U.N. Development Programme (UNDP). 2001. *Human Development Report 2001*. New York and Oxford: Oxford University Press. Available online at: http://www.undp.org/hdr2001.

11 World Bank. 2001b. *World Development Indicators 2001*, on CD-ROM. Washington, DC: The World Bank.

12 World Bank. 2001a.

13 Cohen, N. 1999. "Greening the Internet: Ten Ways E-Commerce Could Affect the Environment." *Environmental Quality Management* 9(1):1-16; Hilty, L. M., P. Gilgen, eds. 2001. *Sustainability in the Information Society*. Marburg, Germany: Metropolis-Verlag; and Wilsdon, J., ed. 2001. *Digital Futures: Living in a dot-com World*. London: Earthscan Publications.

14 UNDP. 2001.

15 Berkhout, F. and J. Hertin. 2001. Organisation for Economic Co-Operation and Development (OECD). "Impacts of Information and Communication Technologies on Environmental Sustainability: Speculations and Evidence," Report to the OECD. United Kingdom: University of Sussex.

■ Total Number of Internet Users: ITU. 2001.

■ Number of PCs, Telephone Lines and Mobile Phones per 1,000 People: World Bank. 2001b.

■ Number of Internet Hosts per 10,000 People: World Bank. 2001b; and World Bank. 2001a.

LABOR

1 World Bank. 1995. *World Development Report 1995: Workers in an Integrating World*. New York: Oxford University Press.

2 U.N. Population Division (UNPD). 2001. *World Population Prospects: The 2000 Revision*. Vol.1: Comprehensive Tables. New York, United Nations; and Rama, M. 2001. "Globalization and Workers in Developing Countries," Online at: http://econ.worldbank.org/files/2870_labor_rama.pdf.

3 The labor force participation rate is the number of people in the labor force as a percentage of the working age population and indicates the supply of labor available and measures the extent of the working-age population that is economically active. The rate tends to be high in less-developed economies but falls as the economy transitions toward higher education, and urbanization and rises again when high development is reached. See International Labour Organization (ILO). 2001. *Key Indicators of Labour Market 2001-2002*, on CD-ROM. International Labor Office, Geneva.

4 UNPD. 2001.

5 Tzannatos, Z. 1998. "Women and Labor Market Changes in the Global Economy: Growth Helps, Inequalities Hurt and Public Policy Matters," Social Protection Discussion Paper Series Discussion Paper 9808 (World Bank, Washington, DC).

6 Organisation for Economic Co-Operation and Development (OECD). 2000. *OECD Employment Outlook, June 2000*. Paris: OECD.

7 Ibid.

8 ILO. 2001.

9 OECD. 2000.

10 ILO. 2001.

11 OECD. 2000.

12 ILO. 2001.

■ Employment-to-Population Ratios: ILO. 2001.

■ Percentage of Labor Force Employed: World Bank. 2000. *World Development Indicators 2000*, on CD-ROM. Washington, DC: The World Bank.

■ Map of Youth Unemployment Rates: ILO. 2001.

■ Non-Resident Visas: U.S. Department of Justice (USDOJ). 2000. *1999 Statistical Yearbook of the Immigration and Naturalization Service*. Washington, DC: USDOJ.

■ H1B Visa Quotas: Organization for Economic Co-Operation and Development (OECD). 2001. *OECD Employment Outlook, June 2001*. Washington, DC: OECD; and U.S. Department of Justice (USDOJ). 2000. 1999 Statistical Yearbook of the Immigration and Naturalization Service. Washington, DC: USDOJ. Available online at: http://www.ins.usdoj.gov/graphics/aboutins/statistics/temp99tables.pf.

Roles and Responsibilities

DEMOCRACY

1 Freedom House. 2001. "Freedom in the World: Number of Democracies 1995-96 and 2000-2001," Online at: http://www.free-domhouse.org/pdf_docs/research/freeworld/2001/map2001.pdf.

2 Ibid.

3 Freedom House. 2001. "Democracy's Century: A Survey of Global Political Change in the 20th Century," Online at: http://www.freedom-house.org/reports/century.pdf.

4 In many countries ratification of an international agreement has no legal implications unless these international commitments are clearly expressed in specific domestic legislation. See U.N. Development Programme (UNDP). 2001. *Human Development Report 2001*. New York and Oxford: Oxford University Press. Available online at: http://www.undp.org/hdr2001.

5 World Bank. 2000. *World Development Report 1999/2000*. Oxford: Oxford University Press. Available online at: http://www.worldbank.org/wdr/2000/fullreport.html.

6 Ibid.

7 Freedom House. 2001. "Freedom in the World: Freedom and Prosperity," Online at: http://www.freedomhouse.org/pdf_docs.

8 World Bank. 1997. *World Development Report 1997*. New York: Oxford University Press.

■ Freedom Rankings, All Countries, 1985-2001: Freedom House. 2001. "Freedom in the World," Online at: http://216.119.183/research/freeworld/2001/tracking.htm.

■ Map of Freedom: Freedom House. 2001. "Freedom in the World: Number of Democracies 1995-96 and 2000-2001," Online at: http://www.freedomhouse.org/research/freeworld/2001/map2001.pdf.

■ Wealth and Freedom Classification: Freedom House. 2001. "Freedom in the World: Number of Democracies 1995-96 and 2000-2001," Online at: http://www.freedomhouse.org/research/freeworld/2001/prosperity.htm.

■ Association of GDP Growth and Policy: World Bank. 1997.

ACCOUNTABILITY

1 Union of International Associations. 1999. "Yearbook of International Organizations," Online at: http://www.uia.org/uiastats/ytb299.htm.

2 Matthews, J. 1997. "Power Shift." *Foreign Affairs* 76(1):50--67.

3 American Association of Fundraising Counsel (AAFRC) Trust for Philanthropy. 1998. *Giving USA 1998*. Indianapolis, Indiana: AAFRC Trust for Philanthropy.

4 Bond, M. 2000. "Special Report: The Backlash Against NGOs." *Prospect* April 52--55. Available online at: http://www.globalpolicy.org/ngos/backlash.htm.

5 U.N. Association of the USA (UNAUSA). "Non-Governmental Organization Affiliation with the U.N.," Online at: http://www.unausa.org/programs/coo/ngo.htm.

6 Global Reporting Initiative (GRI). "GRI Overview," Online at: http://glob-alreporting.org/AboutGRI/Overview.htm; and Global Reporting Initiative (GRI). "Companies using the GRI *Sustainability Reporting Guidelines*," Online at: http://www.globalreporting.org/GRIguidelines/reporters.htm.

7 Social Investment Forum (SIF). 2001. *2001 Report on Socially Responsible Investing Trends in the United States*. Washington, DC: SIF. Available online at: http://www.socialinvest.org/areas/research/trends/2001-Trends.htm.

8 Ibid.

9 Investor Responsibility Research Center (IRRC). 2001a. Social Issues Service. Shareholder Resolution database, 1973-2000. IRRC.

10 Investor Responsibility Research Center (IRRC). 2001b. Personal communication Douglas Cogan.

11 Transparency International (TI). 2001a. "Press Release: New Index Highlights Worldwide Corruption Crisis," Online at: http://www.trans-parency.org/documents/cpi/2001/cpi2001.html#cpi.

12 World Bank. 2001a. *World Development Report 2002 Overview*. Washington, DC: World Bank. Available online at: http://econ.world-bank.org/files/2395_Overview-en.pdf.

13 Strategic Insight (SI). 2001. Strategic Insight Simfund2/MF Database. Strategic Insight.

14 Sparkes, R. "Social Responsible Investment Comes of Age." *Professional Investor,* June 2000, UK. Available online at:

http://www.uksif.org//publications/article-2000-06/content.shtml.

15 Social Investment Forum (SIF). 1999. "1999 Report on Socially Responsible Investing Trends in the United States," Online at: http://www.socialinvest.org/areas/research/trends/1999-Trends.htm.

16 SIF. 2001.

■ Number of Non-Governmental Organizations: Union of International Associations. 1999. "Yearbook of International Organizations," Online at: http://www.uia.org/uiastats/stybv296.htm#1909.

■ U.S. Shareholder Resolutions: IRRC. 2001a.

■ Transparency International's Corruption Perceptions Index: Transparency International (TI). 2001b. "New Index Highlights Worldwide Corruption Crisis," Online at: http://www.transparency.org/documents/cpi/2001/cpi2001.html#cpi.

■ Business Registration Procedures: World Bank. 2001b. *World Development Report 2002*. Washington, D.C: World Bank.

■ Socially Screened Mutual Funds: Strategic Insight. 2001.

PRIVATIZATION

1 Development Assistance Committee (DAC)/Organisation for Economic Co-Operation and Development (OECD). 2001. "Special Factors Explain Official Development Assistance (ODA) Outcome: Development Assistance Committee Announces ODA Figures for 2000," Press Release, April 23. Online at: http://www1.oecd.org/media/release/; United Nations Economic and Social Council. 2001. "Implementing Agenda 21: Report of the UN Secretary General," United Nations; and World Bank. 2000a. "Briefing Papers: Assessing Globalization," PREM Economic Policy Group and Development Economics Group. April 2000. Online at: http://www.worldbank.org/html/extdr/pb/globaliza-tion/paper1.htm.

2 World Bank. 2001a. *World Development Indicators 2001*, on CD-ROM. Washington, DC: The World Bank.

3 World Bank. 2001b. *Global Development Finance 2001*. Washington, DC: World Bank. Available online at: http://www.worldbank.org/prospects/gdf2001/vol1.htm.

4 World Bank Group International Finance Corporation (IFC). 1997. "Trends in Private Investment in Developing Countries Statistics for 1970-1995," Discussion Paper Number 31 (The World Bank, Washington, DC). Available online at: http://www.ifc.org/economics/pubs/dp31/PRIVPI.htm.

5 World Bank. 2001b.

6 World Bank. 2001c. *World Development Indicators 2001*. Washington, DC: The World Bank.

7 World Bank. 2001b.

8 Organisation for Economic Co-Operation and Development (OECD). 2001. *Recent Privatization Trends*. Paris: OECD. Available online at: http://www.oecd.org/pdf/M00007000/M00007473.pdf.

9 Roger, N. 1999. *Recent Trends in Private Participation in Infrastructure*. Public Policy for the Private Sector. Note 196, Sept. 1999, The World Bank. Available online at: http://www.worldbank.org/html/fpd/notes/196/196roger.pdf.

10 OECD. 2001.

11 World Bank. 2000b. *Global Development Finance 2000*. Washington, DC: World Bank. Available online at: http://www.worldbank.org/prospects/gdf2000/CH2--34-55.pdf; and World Bank. 2001b.

■ Foreign Investment Flows to Developing Countries: World Bank. 2000b; and World Bank. 2001b.

■ Private Capital Flows: World Bank. 2001c.

■ Privatization by Major Sectors: World Bank. 2001b.

■ Investment in Private or Partial-Private Infrastructure: Roger, N. 1999.

■ Global Amounts Raised from Privatization: OECD. 2001.

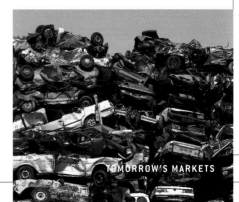

BUSINESS SUSTAINABILITY

Below are a selection of publications on topics related to how business is responding to global economic, environmental and social trends to create shareholder and stakeholder value.

General Sustainability

- Anderson, R.C. 1998. *Mid-Course Correction: Toward a Sustainable Enterprise: The Interface Model.* Atlanta: Peregrinzilla Press.

- Andriof, J. and M. McIntosh. 2001. *Perspectives on Corporate Citizenship.* Sheffield, UK: Greenleaf Publishing.

- Arnold, M.B. and R.M. Day. 1998. *The Next Bottom Line: Making Sustainable Development Tangible.* Washington, DC: World Resources Institute.

- Elkington, J. 1997. *Cannibals with Forks: The Triple Bottom Line of 21st Century Business.* Oxford: Capstone Publishing Limited.

- Elkington, J. 2001. *The Chrysalis Economy: How Citizen CEOs and Corporations Can Fuse Values and Value Creation.* Oxford: Capstone Publishing Ltd.

- Frankel, C. 1998. *In Earth's Company: Business, Environment, and the Challenge of Sustainability.* Gabriola Island, Canada: New Society Publishers.

- Freeman, R.E., J. Pierce, and R. Dodd. 2000. *Environmentalism and the New Logic of Business.* New York: Oxford University Press.

- Harvard Business Review. 1999. *Harvard Business Review on Business & the Environment.* Boston: Harvard Business School Press.

- Hawken, P. 1993. *The Ecology of Commerce: A Declaration of Sustainability.* New York: Harper-Business.

- Hawken, P. et al. 1999. *Natural Capitalism: Creating the Next Industrial Revolution.* Boston: Little, Brown and Company.

- Hoffman, A.J. 2000. *Competitive Environmental Strategy: A Guide to the Changing Business Landscape.* Washington, DC: Kogan Page.

- Hoffman, A.J. 2001. *From Heresy to Dogma: An Institutional History of Corporate Environmentalism.* Stanford. Stanford University Press.

- Nattrass, B. and M. Altomare. 1999. *The Natural Step for Business.* Gabriola Island, Canada: New Society Publishers.

- Piasecki, B., K.A. Fletcher, and F. Mendelson. 1999. *Environmental Management and Business Strategy: Leadership Skills for the 21st Century.* New York: John Wiley.

- Post, J.E., A.T. Lawrence, and J. Weber. 2001. *Business and Society: Corporate Strategy, Public Policy, and Ethics.* Boston: McGraw Hill.

- Schmidheiny, S. 1992. *Changing Course: A Global Business Perspective on Development and the Environment.* London: MIT Press Ltd.

- SustainAbility and U.N. Environment Programme (UNEP). 2001. *Buried Treasure: Uncovering the Business Case for Corporate Sustainability.* London, UK.

- Welford, R. and R. Starkey, eds. *The Earthscan Reader in Business and Sustainable Development.* London: Earthscan Publications. 2001.

- Willums, J.O. 1998. *The Sustainable Business Challenge: A Briefing for Tomorrow's Business Leaders.* Sheffield, UK: Greenleaf Publishing.

Strategies for Sustainability

- Buchholz, R. A. 1998. *Principles of Environmental Management: The Greening of Business.* Upper Saddle River, New Jersey: Prentice Hall.

- Charter, M. and U. Tischner, eds. 2001. *Sustainable Solutions: Developing Products and Services for the Future.* Sheffield: Greenleaf.

- Fussler, C. and P. James. 1996. *Driving Eco-Innovation: A Breakthrough Discipline for Innovation and Sustainability.* London: Pitman Publishing

- Holliday, C. and J. Pepper. 2001. *Sustainability through the Market: Seven Keys to Success.* World Business Council for Sustainable Development.

- McIntosh, M., D. Leipziger, K. Jones, and G. Coleman. 1998. *Corporate Citizenship: Successful Strategies for Responsible Companies.* London: Pitman Publishing.

- Ottman, J.A. 1998. *Green Marketing: Opportunity for Innovation.* Chicago: NTC Business Books.

- Reinhardt, F.L. 2000. *Down to Earth: Applying Business Principles to Environmental Management.* Boston, Massachusetts: Harvard Business School Press.

- Roome, N.J. ed. 1998. *Sustainability Strategies for Industry: The Future of Corporate Practice.* Washington, DC: Island Press.

- Sagawa, S. and E. Segal. 2000. *Common Interest, Common Good: Creating Value through Business and Social Sector Partnerships.* Boston, Massachusetts: Harvard Business School Press.

- Schmidheiny, S., F.J. Zorraquin. 1998. *Financing Change: The Financial Community, Eco-Efficiency, and Sustainable Development.* Cambridge, Massachusetts: MIT Press.

- Svendsen, A. 1999. *The Stakeholder Strategy: Profiting from Collaborative Business Relationships.* Francisco, CA: Berrett-Koehler Publishers.

- Wheeler, D., and M. Sillanpää. 1997. *The Stakeholder Corporation: The Body Shop: Blueprint for Maximizing Stakeholder Value.* London: Pitman Publishing.

- World Business Council for Sustainable Development (WBCSD). 2000. *Eco-efficiency: Creating More Value with Less Impact.* Geneva: WBCSD.

Measurement and Reporting

- Bennet, M. and P. James, eds. 1999. *Sustainable Measures: Evaluation and Reporting of Environmental and Social Performance.* Sheffield, UK: Greenleaf Publishing Limited.

- Ditz, D., J. Ranganathan, and R.D. Banks. 1995. *Green Ledgers: Case Studies in Corporate Environmental Accounting.* Washington, DC: World Resources Institute.

- Epstein, M.J. 1996. *Measuring Corporate Environmental Performance: Best Practices for Costing and Managing an Effective Environmental Strategy.* New York: McGraw-Hill.

- Global Reporting Initiative (GRI). 2000. *Sustainability Reporting Guidelines on Economic, Environmental and Social Performance.* Boston: GRI.

- Jeucken, M. 2001. *Sustainable Finance & Banking: The Financial Sector and the Future of the Planet.* London: Earthscan.

- U.N. Environment Programme (UNEP) and SustainAbility. 1999. *Engaging Stakeholders 1999: The Social Reporting Report.* London, UK: SustainAbility Ltd.